Handwriting Problems in the Secondary School

Rosemary Sassoon

Handwriting Problems in the Secondary School

Rosemary Sassoon

Paul Chapman Publishing

First published 2006

Paul Chapman Publishing
A SAGE Publications Company
1 Oliver's Yard
55 City Road
London EC1Y 1SP

SAGE Publications Inc
2455 Teller Road
Thousand Oaks, California 91320

SAGE Publications India Pvt Ltd
B-42, Panchsheel Enclave
Post Box 4109
New Delhi 110 017

Library of Congress Control Number: 2006929011

A catalogue record for this book is available from the British Library

ISBN-10 1-4129-2888-5   ISBN-13 978-1-4129-2888-5
ISBN-10 1-4129-2889-3   ISBN-13 978-1-4129-2889-2 (pbk)

Illustrations by Pat Savage from photographs by the author
Designed and typeset by Blacker Design, East Grinstead RH19 4LY
Printed in Great Britain by The Cromwell Press Ltd, Trowbridge, Wiltshire
Printed on paper from sustainable resources

Contents

Contents

Part 3

Introduction

A CONSIDERABLE PROPORTION of pupils leave primary school unable to write sufficiently well to deal with the demands of secondary school. It may be that they have been inadequately or inappropriately taught, or they may have a physical problem, diagnosed or not, that has inhibited their learning. It may even be that they have made up their minds that handwriting is a redundant skill in the age of computers.

Whatever the reason, it is a great waste of potential. Unfortunately society still tends to judge people of whatever age by the standard of their written trace. To writers themselves the constant reminder of failure every time they put pen to paper is demoralising and likely to result in reluctant learners and under-achieving adults.

Handwriting is still needed for certain important tasks, though perhaps viewed more as a tool for creativity than as an end in itself.

The conventional neat, inevitably slow, writing of the past is not so much of a priority. Most show writing may now be produced by computer. A fast note-taking hand, however, is vital in secondary school, also a slightly more legible but equally speedy form of writing for examinations. It may be quite a while before computers can be used in these and other similar circumstances.

Handwriting problems differ from other educational problems. The written trace is the result of the movement of the hand when it is in contact with the paper. It is a fair indication, therefore, of the state of mind and body of the writer at the time of writing. This is useful for diagnosis but this personal aspect makes it so hard to deal with older pupils already confirmed in their personal mark. To criticise their handwriting can seem like an attack on their very person. If done without sensitivity it may make matters worse. Without understanding it is unlikely to succeed.

Handwriting problems are seldom straightforward by the time pupils reach secondary school. No two problems are exactly the same, however similar the written sample, and no two pupils' characters or aspirations or capabilities are either. We have definite expectations in our educational system and even in society. Only too often those who do not conform are seen as problems. Moreover our system seems prone to criticise rather than praise which further isolates those who do not or cannot come up to expectation. Some pupils could be just different, and their differences reflected in their writing, rather than their being problematic.

Without underestimating any serious problems that some children may be facing, part of the situation that we find ourselves in today has arisen from the desire to label children. Standardised tests may be used to justify these labels. These are seldom any use to the individuals involved, and with handwriting, seldom result in an accurate enough diagnosis. With complex problems we need to think of the individual not the label. Labelling often precludes further diagnostic techniques, where a solution may be found.

When questioned about their handwriting pupils often answer that there is no problem and they can write perfectly well – the problem is in the eye of their teacher or parent. They say that their handwriting would serve them quite well enough if only they were left alone instead of constantly being criticised. This may or may not be true as it is notoriously difficult to self- diagnose. It is worth, however, taking notice of this because pressure and criticism fuel tension. Tension alone can distort an otherwise acceptable script, thus mimicking many of the symptoms of more serious conditions such as a tremor.

The worries of constant testing during the primary years, and in the case of private schools, intense competition and worries of common entrance, compound this tension. Hands become tense, echoing the tension throughout their bodies, so that pupils can become unable to write. This is a kind of juvenile writer's cramp but indefensible in children so young. Who is at fault? Ambitious parents, who may well think they are doing their best for their children, or schools avid for successful ratings, or once more thinking that they are only trying to get the best out of their pupils? It is hard to tell, but it is obvious who are the victims – the children.

This is why this project has been planned in several parts. In Part 2 the half page, photocopiable pupil material has an innovative purpose (in addition to being helpful to teachers). That is to allow pupils, in the more straightforward matters of letterforms, to see examples of problem handwriting that perhaps is similar to their own. To realise why it might be hard to read, and perhaps to laugh at the faults that appear only too obvious in the illustrations. This may lead them to self-correct without any outside pressure.

As well as the letterform aspects there are matters such as posture, paper position and the vexed issue of pen hold. They are illustrated and explained in such a way to suggest what steps might be taken to benefit individuals and invite experimentation.

In each of these areas it is difficult for older pupils to alter entrenched habits without motivation – and in handwriting perhaps the best motivation comes from within. To understand a problem can be half way to solving it.

The Companion Website

A companion website for this book can be found at www.sagepub.co.uk/sassoon. On the site you will find all of the photocopiable pupil material from Part 2, available in pdf format. This will give you the flexibility to be able to print relevant pages for pupil use, or to print out the whole section and compile it into a booklet for pupils to work through. Pupils can also visit the site directly to access the pages themselves. Also on the website is a range of links to other useful sources of information and help, and more details of Rosemary Sassoon's work.

Part 1

Part 1

THIS BOOK OUTLINES the various aspects of handwriting problems, offering guidance to teachers on a diagnostic system and techniques to develop their observation and practice.

Secondary teachers may not have covered much about handwriting issues during their training. It is first necessary to begin by explaining the factors involved in the initial teaching of handwriting because some pupils may not have been taught enough about handwriting and have to go back to basics before they can improve. This part will have the following sections:

Issues concerning letterforms:

- Movement
- Height differentials
- Two sets of letters
- Word or letter spacing
- Handwriting models
- Speed
- A balanced view of joining

Issues affecting how we write

- The effects of school furniture on posture
- Pens and pen hold and paper position
- Understanding left handedness
- Tension
- Vision and pain

Other issues

- Presentation
- Talking to parents
- Severe problems ignored or misdiagnosed
- Handwriting in a multicultural context

■ Issues in letterforms

Movement

The movement of writing refers to the way letters are formed, their point of entry and direction of stroke. This is sometimes called the ductus of letters, from the Latin 'to lead'. It is also referred to as the trajectory. These terms emphasise the dynamic aspect of letters rather than just their static shape.

The correct movement of letters enables handwriting to remain reasonably legible even when written at speed or carelessly. It also enables the hand that writes to move smoothly and efficiently across the page.

Ideally, children should be taught the correct movement of letters when they first learn to write. Unfortunately this vital part of skill training is often ignored in the rush to literacy and in the interest of getting children to express themselves on paper.

Once an incorrect movement becomes automated it is increasingly difficult for the writer to alter the habit. This is the consequence of writing being a motor skill. It is unlikely that movement faults will be corrected by themselves. That is why the first check for secondary school pupils must be for letters with an incorrect movement.

Height differentials

The different height of letters and their relationship to each other affects the word shape. This contributes to the way mature or fast writing can be easily deciphered.

Where letters have inadequate ascending or descending strokes, or where they are not correctly aligned in relation to each other pupils deserve an explanation of why it is important for them to change. Like all aspects of personal letters it may not be easy for the writer to alter an entrenched habit.

Two sets of letters

Capitals and small letters may still confuse some pupils, or they may purposely be using them inappropriately. They need an explanation in the context of usage in our writing system. It is all too easy to forget these different discriminations that we as adults take for granted. Few people can give pupils a logical explanation as to why there are two sets of letters in our writing system. The history of our alphabet is a long and complex story. If you are interested you can find all about it in the *Encyclopaedia Britannica*. Children, however, deserve a simple explanation as to why the shapes of our two sets of letters are different. Our hand written letters have developed gradually during the past two thousand years from the Roman cursives. These are very hard to decipher today unless you are a paleographer. The form of capital letters has remained virtually unchanged from the formal letters inscribed on the Trajan Column in Rome in AD 114. Their straight strokes had evolved to make it easier to inscribe letters on stone or marble. We write them with pencil and pen today.

Word and letter spacing

Word spacing is related to writing size so there cannot be a general rule that dictates what is optimum to make a text easily legible. There is, however, one factor that often needs addressing that is the direct consequence of a practice often used when first teaching young children. Infants are often told to use their thumb to measure the space between words. This may be a convenient explanation at the age of five, but thumbs grow and writing gets smaller. Surprisingly the concept seems embedded in some older pupils' consciousness. The consequence of extra wide word spaces results in rivers of white space down the page.

Today, most pupils are familiar with keyboards, where a word space is the same same size as a letter. It is more or less the same rule for written letters.

There are no specific rules concerning letter spacing. It should be a matter of common sense but there still can be a few problems that continue into the teenage years. These are usually caused by the forms children learned when young. If they learned straight print script letters and then taught themselves to join, their joining strokes might always be jagged and uneven, affecting letter spacing. At the other extreme some pupils, usually with poor coordination, may have developed exaggerated joining strokes which space letters very widely, sometimes suggesting an additional letter.

Quite a different problem arises when pupils have never learned to join their letters. Instead, they may pack them close together to disguise the fact.

This can make certain words difficult to decipher. Uneven letter or word spacing is one of those indicators that help us to understand a pupil's particular problem. It can indicate hesitation sometimes caused by difficulty over spelling, for example, or maybe extreme tension from any other cause in the school or home environment.

Other factors

There are two other aspects of our writing system that may contribute to handwriting problems. Usually they have been dealt with before reaching secondary school, but occasionally they persist. One is the actual direction of writing – from left to right. The easiest movement for most left handers is from right to left. You can observe this from watching the way they usually cross their 't's. For a few left handers this poses a considerable problem, although the majority learn to adapt. The difficulty can manifest itself in several ways. one is the slowing down of writing as the writer has to fight the tendency to write each word from right to left. This may also show in certain letters being reversed, usually at the end of a word as the writer relaxes.

The other factor is mirror image. Some of the letters in our alphabet are mirror images of each other. Those pupils with perceptual troubles may be unable to perceive and produce the differences between such letters. It is not only the usual confusing pair of 'b' and 'd' to be aware of. Some pupils find the same difficulty with 'u' and 'n'. None of these problems should be confused with dyslexia, and should be treated sympathetically.

All of these issues are dealt with separately in the next section.

Handwriting Models

The UK, unlike most other countries, has a long tradition of respecting individual schools' right to choose their own handwriting model. This concept is central to the National Curriculum so contributes to the variety of styles found in secondary schools. A model may be necessary in the early stages of handwriting instruction, but the question is what model, and should it be the same for all children? The problem with a national model, or even a strict school model, is that the emphasis inevitably falls on the copying of the details of the model rather than the automation of consistent personal handwriting. It may be thought simpler to teach children to conform to a strict model. Their work looks more attractive when put up on display. But is it the way for pupils to acquire the fast efficient handwriting that they need today? Flexible and informed teaching is needed to guide pupils at a vulnerable age.

When any model is kept for too long or taught too strictly, young writers do not have the opportunity to experiment. Experimentation leads to personal letters, and to the establishment of the slant and proportion that suits individual hands and characters. This is the way to automated and consistent handwriting when the pupil can concentrate on the content of the written work instead of worrying about details of the school model.

A more liberal attitude to the model does not necessarily lead to untidy or illegible handwriting. Several countries, where previously national models were enforced, have had to revise their curricula. They have found that their pupils frequently could not speed up their writing in secondary school, and reverted to separate letters. In some cases this was because they had been taught continuous cursive which is notoriously difficult to speed up.

It is unlikely that a secondary school would impose a definite model, but teachers have to face the consequences of multiple styles, some effective some not. Some are the consequence of taught models and some of personal experimentation and development. It is almost always counter-productive to force a pupil to alter from a perfectly adequate style to that approved by a new school or teacher, however tempting it may appear. By style I mean a different slant or proportion of letters or other different details. This does not include helping a pupil to start changing from simple printed letters to those with exit strokes in preparation to joining up.

There may be times when pupils have been taught a model or developed a style that patently hinders their progress. This is sometimes the case with an exaggerated italic or when older pupils still use the entry strokes to their letters that they had been taught in an attempt to train them to write an old fashioned continuous cursive.

In such cases advice may be needed, but there are two things to remember. Pupils may be very defensive of their personal style. On the other hand teachers must always be on guard against their own personal stylistic prejudices. Gentle explanation of the advantages and disadvantages is the best way forward. This should help pupils to understand and to gradually adapt their script. If they choose not to alter their handwriting, then it is not right to try and force them.

Speed

There cannot be an optimum level of speed at any stage. Too many other factors are involved. The teacher's role, by the end of junior school, should be to equip their pupils, by whatever means, with a fast enough hand to deal with the next stage of education. When pupils first enter secondary school the need for speeding up may not immediately be obvious. Different written tasks, however, will soon be introduced and it is important that everyone understands that there are different levels of writing suitable for different tasks.

Firstly, everyone must understand that speed is likely to affect neatness and therefore legibility at any level. On the other hand, when speed is necessary it could be said that to spend time raising handwriting to an unnecessarily high level for any particular task is a waste of time. Most adults work on that principle automatically, but what does it mean to the average school child? It means that first drafts of essays or notes can be roughly written as long as they are decipherable to the writer, but French homework, for instance, will need even more care than an English exercise, because so much depends on the accuracy of single letters. Therefore the writer may have to slow down.

When children start secondary school they will need a fast handwriting for note-taking and increased homework. It could all be summed up by saying that a scribble is as vital as slow, neat handwriting, and those pupils who demonstrate the most difference between their levels of handwriting indicate that they are the most flexible and efficient, making best use of the available time.

Handwriting is a tool for creativity and reacts with other cognitive skills. If a pupil has spelling or other problems with literacy then this will affect speed, however efficient their motor skills and letterforms may be. Handwriting exercises, therefore, are unlikely to be any help. On the other hand efficient thinkers who make the point of any written work succinct and as brief as possible will have less need of speed. These factors illustrate how impractical general speed tests are likely to be.

Speed tests of the informal kind are useful in encouraging children to keep their pens on the paper and to join up their letters. Later they help pupils to bring out the most efficient joins and individual shortcuts in their personal handwriting. An informed teacher can be crucial in interpreting such experiments. A rough scribble can often be shown as the beginning of mature handwriting. The tight, neat but childish letterforms that still adhere to the taught model are only holding the writer back.

A balanced view of joining

As many handwriting problems are caused by joining up too much as by not joining at all. With modern pens and the way we hold them pen lifts are needed in the middle of long words so that the hand can move comfortably along the line as it writes. This results in more relaxed letters and joins. Some primary school children relate that if they were to do this in class they would be 'told off' for not joining every letter all the time. Sometimes they are so desperate that they take a pen lift and then disguise it with a false joining stroke afterwards. Yet joins are meant to facilitate fast efficient mature handwriting. They are not meant as an instrument of torture.

Children need to learn how all the letters join, and then to use them as appropriate. Joining letters is not a complex matter, and I often wonder why it becomes such an emotive issue. All that is necessary, when

children can produce basic separate letters with the correct movement, is to keep the pencil on the paper when moving from the end of one letter to the beginning of the next. The National Curriculum document recognises this when it encourages early joins, rather than the retention of neat separate letters until the age of seven or beyond. If your pupils are not joining up when they reach secondary schools, then after you have checked their letters for movement faults, explain how simple it all is and encourage them to join. You can start with the simplest joins first: those that join from the baseline.

Joining will be most difficult for those who pride themselves on their neat print script. That is why it is better that all infants are taught letters that have integral exit strokes from the start. The abrupt letters of print script result in real difficulties. They mean that children have to take the pressure off the terminal of the letter at the baseline, and change direction at the same time, before the letters and can flow and join. Letters with exits promote a more relaxed hand position, movement and pressure, all of which lead to spontaneous joins along the baseline. It is undeniable that children's first attempts at joined up cannot be as neat as their separate letters. Later on such pupils may find it difficult to relax their self-set standard. It is up to the teacher to explain the advantages of joins, and to have a balanced attitude to the level of joining.

Roughly speaking, round letters join less easily than oval slanting ones, which permit simpler ligatures to some letters. This does not mean that all children should or could be made to write oval slanting letters. On the whole, large writing needs more rests than small writing, and left-handers may need more pen lifts than right-handers, but it is not an exact count of how many letters before a pen lift, nor precisely which letters should join and which should not. The complexity of the strokes within the letters and their position within the word often influence the frequency of pen lifts.

Most adults lift their pen from the paper every few letters. Why, therefore, should we insist that children should not be allowed to do likewise? In the last century quills were used. Then it was inadvisable to stop in the middle of a word in case the pen spluttered ink all over the page. In those days, however, writers were carefully trained not to rest the whole hand on the table while writing, but to balance lightly on their little finger. This allowed the pen to glide easily along the line, but it is not easy, and certainly is not a realistic way of dealing with modern pens.

Instruction is meant to give pupils efficient handwriting that works as effortlessly as possible for them. If it is beautiful then that is an added benefit, but as long as it is legible and preferably consistent, as well as being capable of being speeded up to the almost impossible speed needed for note-taking and passing examinations, then you, the teacher, need not be too worried. Children do not willingly write badly. Many of the pupils who face daily criticism of their writing (joined or not) are so tense and unhappy about it that this in itself is enough to distort letters and invite even further loss of marks and derogatory remarks at the bottom of their work. If something is really wrong with their handwriting then pupils need informed diagnosis and help. Otherwise, try a bit of praise instead of criticism, it often works wonderfully well.

■ Issues in writing posture

The term writing posture is defined not only as how pupils sit but includes pen hold, paper position and other issues that concern how, rather than what, a pupil writes. These tend to be inter-related. So far the letters have been emphasised but it is also important to consider the writer's body. Have you ever walked behind the rows of desks and observed the tortured postures of so many of your pupils when they are engrossed in their work? Why do we allow this? Why do the pupils themselves not complain because surely it cannot benefit either the taking in of information or the writing down of it to be so uncomfortable? An idiosyncratic posture can be an indicator of various conditions. As an aid to diagnosis an unusual posture may indicate visual or other problems. See page 12.

School furniture and posture

Relating furniture to posture, and posture to handwriting, it becomes clear that it may not be possible to write well unless the body is properly placed and the arm able to move freely. I can sympathise with schools with overstretched budgets, or those whose furniture purchases are dictated by central buying. However, it might be possible to organise matters so that the few over-large, or very small pupils have provision made for them. It is often only a matter of being flexible about the use of the different sizes of furniture that are usually to be found in different parts of most schools.

The health and physiques of a few pupils may have already been damaged by the extended use of inappropriate furniture in their junior schools. Their bodies, too flexible to feel pain, may have became twisted instead. On the other hand, I have seen enlightened primary schools, where three sizes of chairs and desks are ranged from the back to the front of the class, allowing for the different builds of their pupils. This is more difficult in a secondary school, where pupils are constantly on the move. One idea is to bring this problem into the open and discuss it with all concerned – including the pupils. Making pupils aware of their posture and how furniture and other factors affect their comfort, and perhaps alleviate their discomfort, may be the best way forward.

Years ago most school desks were set at a slant. For centuries, from monks in scriptoria to Victorian clerks, people always wrote on slanting surfaces. Such desks may be out of fashion, but it is worth thinking about trying out the benefits of a slant for those with certain physical problems. Anyone with a tremor, from whatever cause, will benefit because their arm will then be better supported. The degree of appropriate slant will differ from person to person. This does not necessarily imply the need for expensive equipment.

An atlas propped on a couple of books, or even the ever-present loose leaf file with the fatter end further from their body, gives some support. These can provide a comfortable slant without attracting too much attention. Such assistance costs little or nothing, and can make a real difference to pupils' performance as well as comfort.

Incidentally, a board supported on the lap, propped against the table, not only demonstrates how comfortable a slant can be but is useful for a secondary pupil who is severely restricted in height. One such boy in secondary school, whose height was equivalent to a six year old, was equipped with a polystyrene board which he carried by a strap. This enabled him to work in any classroom without the trouble of special furniture.

Some specific furniture or writing surfaces can adversely affect handwriting. Several sets of pupils have described how the high stools and damaged surface of the tables in their school laboratories have caused trouble and unfairly invited criticism of their written work.

Writing posture consists of more than sitting posture and desk or chair height. If writers are to be able to hold the pen comfortably, yet still see what they are doing, they need to place the paper to the side of the hand that writes – right-handers to their right side and left-handers, even more importantly, to their left side. This brings us back to furniture because it means that there must be enough space on the desk or table to make this possible.

The 'modern' hexagonal tables, which are widely used in infant schools, provide only enough space for the paper to be centrally spaced in front of each young writer. This space is so limited that there is not enough room for children to use their other hand to support the paper.

You may have to explain this to some of your pupils who now might have sufficient space and encourage them to alter their paper position so they can sit comfortably, hold their pen happily, and see what they are writing. Even this seemingly simple and beneficial alteration is not always easy. Every aspect of the physical act of writing becomes automated and difficult to change. Without motivation, changes such as those involving paper position or pen hold, for instance, may be almost impossible for a pupil who has written in a particular way for several years.

Pens and pen hold

This is an emotive and often explosive subject in some classrooms. First there is the writing implement itself to consider. Pen and pen hold are interrelated, as are the resulting letterforms. Throughout history, as pens developed and letterforms altered in consequence, the writing masters of the day paid attention at each stage to different ways of holding the pen. In the last few decades radical alterations have taken place in the design of pens, yet few people have considered that we ought to develop an alternative pen hold. This is an area that I have researched quite thoroughly,

In the second part of the book some of the unconventional pen holds seen in classrooms today are illustrated and discussed. The suggested cause of these pen holds is that modern pens need to be held at a more upright angle than traditional pens and pencils. That is sometimes difficult to achieve with the traditional tripod grip. Although they may appear awkward not all unconventional pen holds slow the writer down or become painful.

What suits one hand may not be best for another, so not all pupils should be made to use the same writing implement. For instance, I would not necessarily prescribe a fountain pen for everyone. Fountain pens may be a distinct disadvantage for left handers. The suitability of a fountain pen for any particular writer may be dependent on the width of nib or the efficiency of the ink flow. Today most pens are sold in packaging so there is no opportunity to test them before buying. A parent can make an expensive mistake.

Modern pens are here to stay, and the better ones have qualities that are well suited to the kind of writing and circumstances of writing that face our students today. A good quality fountain pen, with satisfactory ink flow, a nib suited to the individual's writing, and a barrel that fits his or her hand comfortably might be best for some children, but not all. Wherever possible a free choice of writing implements is best. It would be a good idea to allow your pupils to experiment with various kinds of pens to find out what suits them and their handwriting. Simple pen preference tests are interesting for all concerned, and are the best way of finding out what best suits your particular group of pupils.

As a simple illustration of the fact that personal choice of pen point, barrel size or shape, length or even material is individual, try asking colleagues or pupils to change pens with their neighbours. What one person finds best to write with, the next one might heartily dislike.

Different pens also require different pen holds. Different hands need slightly different pen holds to be comfortable as well. There is a very efficient alternative pen hold that works better with modern pens than the traditional tripod grip. It is probably more relaxed and certainly less likely to be painful, when used under pressure for long periods of writing

The alternative penhold

such as at examination time. It is easier to illustrate it than to describe. Do try it. You may not like it yourself, but it may work exceptionally well for some of your pupils.

If pupils are able to write fast enough to keep up, without pain and without distorting the letterforms, then, however awkward their pen hold may look to you it may be best to leave the situation alone. Unless you can provide a good enough reason to motivate them to alter, then you are unlikely to succeed, and quite likely their solution suits them better than yours. The best that you can do is to explain that if that pen hold should begin to slow them down as the demand for speed increases, or if it begins to cause them discomfort, then they should experiment themselves to find something better.

As mentioned earlier all aspects of writing posture are inter-related. Pen holds can seldom be dealt with in isolation. Many twisted pen holds have arisen because of inappropriate paper position, so the paper will need to go further to the side of the writing hand, and may need to be slanted too, before the pen hold can be altered. Sometimes this will afford the writers with a better view of their work and allow an uncomfortable twisted wrist to unwind.

Other pen holds are caused by the general tension of the writer and can be seen to alter as the pupil relaxes. Without real motivation (it sounds cruel but the best motivation is to alleviate pain), it will be hard for writers to alter their pen hold. It all comes down to the physical difficulty of changing a learned and automated action.

Understanding left-handedness

Some left-handers never have any problems with writing, drawing or any other precision tasks, but others have considerable difficulties with a writing system that undoubtedly works better for right-handers. Left-handers need practical help from the start to develop strategies to deal with their special requirements. The most important and often neglected advice concerns paper position. If left-handers are taught to place their paper to their left side many difficulties can be avoided. This allows them to see what they are doing, or have written, without bending their bodies sideways or twisting their wrists over the top of the line of writing. It also helps to avoid smudged work.

If the paper is to go to the left side, then there must be enough space, and when left-handers sit next to their right-handed friends, then it should be to the side where they do not jog each other as they write. Classrooms are often organised for right-handers, so it is necessary to ensure that left-handers have enough light to see what they are doing. In the early stages children need softish pencils that do not dig into the paper, not hard sharp points.

Modern fibre-tipped pens are ideal for left-handers. They move easily and do not smudge. Fountain pens can make writing difficult for those who are left handed but some secondary schools still insist on their use. All these practical points are quite simple to organise, but can make considerable differences in children's ability to write and to their whole attitude to written tasks.

Many left-handers have writing that slopes backwards. This should not matter unless the slant is excessive and affects the legibility of the writing. Some teachers find a backwards slanting writing somehow reprehensible, and criticise children without realising that slant is a result of how the pen is manipulated. A forward slant can be difficult for young left-handers. The easiest way to produce a forward slant is for the writer to twist (invert) the wrist. This frequently invites more criticism.

One solution might be that there could be slightly backward slanting models for those who otherwise would always be striving to attain the (almost) impossible.

Certain letters are particularly difficult for left-handers. The worst are 'f' and 's' because they involve a change of direction. Writers can be helped to simplify these letters and to find the way of writing them that is easiest and most economical for them to write. Working together to design personal letters is a particularly satisfying exercise, bridging the 'them and us' situation that often arises in handwriting criticism.

If right-handers had to spend a day or so using their left hands then it might be easier for them to understand what it feels like to be in that position permanently. In countries where the curriculum sets specific guidelines for dealing with left-handers fewer problems are reported. This suggests that many left-handers who fail to achieve their optimum are victims of an unsympathetic system.

There are also more complex problems. These are concerned with directionality, a little understood aspect of our physical make up. A left-hander usually draws a line more easily from right to left, so, for example, 't' and 'f' will be crossed in that direction. This may prevent left-handers from using some of the shortcuts available to right-handers but that is no real problem. The trouble arises when the right-to-left directional pull is so strong that the writer finds difficulty in proceeding in the correct direction within separate letters or between them, and occasionally within whole words.

Young children may persist in starting at the wrong place and writing in the wrong direction, resulting in mirror writing. Later on joining may be difficult. Left-handers' difficulties may be misinterpreted as being slow at writing, or just untidy. Their problems can often only be understood by observing them in the act of writing. One unfortunate left-hander described how he could neither control nor understand his urge to go clockwise around a letter and backwards. This always happened when he tried to write neatly and slowly to please his teacher. If he wrote fast the momentum seemed to carry him in the right direction, but then he was criticised for untidy writing.

If you have such a child in your class ask him or her to explain the way he or she feels, and how strong the urge is to go in the 'wrong' direction. This is the best way for you both to learn how to understand such problems. Sympathy, not criticism, is needed. Some children, once they understand the problem, can themselves develop techniques to overcome this directional pull, but occasionally it is so strong that all attempts fail and a word processor may be the answer. By that time the pupil may scan and even spell from right to left, a problem that is hard to diagnose and even harder to know how to help.

Tension

Handwriting is not just a simple matter of letters, neat or untidy. It is a physical act that involves not only the hand but the whole body. It interacts with other cognitive tasks, and above all is affected by, and in turn reflects, the writer's emotions and attitudes. This makes handwriting an ideal diagnostic tool. You as their teacher are in an ideal position to chart the ups and downs of your pupils through their handwriting. Glancing through their books it is sometimes possible to see which subjects are boring or perhaps stressful.

Tension affects the arm and hand as it does the whole body. As tensions build up, handwriting deteriorates. It may be that examinations are near, but the tension might just as easily indicate the breakup of their parents' marriage, a bereavement or a bout of bullying. Tension is an indicator, and a little gentle questioning may discover the cause; then an explanation may defuse a difficult situation. You may know the reason, but may be unable to do much about it, other than offering sympathy. It could be a matter for a referral to other professionals. However, by recognising the cause of the tense writing rather than criticising the distorted result, an injustice is avoided.

An unhappy child will not be able to avoid the uneven or jagged strokes that he or she cannot control, just as poor spellers cannot achieve fluent writing as long as they are uncertain of which letter should come next. An intelligent child with an awkward body may never achieve the smooth writing that comes easily to others, however hard he (it is more often boys who suffer this way) may try to please.

That term 'awkward body' can cover many problems, dyspraxia being one. Having had a stroke myself I would make a special plea for those who can write slowly but not speed up. Many kinds of marginal brain damage make this impossible. Making any limb speed up in such circumstances may cause confusion even panic. This will only be reflected in a confused trace. Sometimes a laptop is the best solution – but do not blame the pupil.

Vision and pain

It is surprising how often eyes are at fault when pupils are having difficulty with reading or writing. It is often caused by more complex conditions than simple long- or short-sightedness that should have been picked up by the school nurse. It is, however, always worth checking as some children in Primary School can miss the regular tests through absence or illness.

When pupils are engrossed in their school work it is often relatively easy to spot those with obscure visual problems. Look for those who hold their heads at an awkward angle, those who keep losing their place, those with uneven margins or word spacing. If you watch their eye movements you can get more of an idea of what is wrong. There are plenty of reasons why pupils might be good at oral work and poor at written exercises. One of these is the difficulty of having no leading eye. It is quite common and only means that both eyes are equally strong. Our eyes work better in literacy tasks when one leads and the other follows. Such children have specific problems with the central area of a page, where they are likely to change from using one eye to the other. These pupils will not be happy on the computer, and they may have trouble adding columns of figures.

Other pupils report (if asked) that they find difficulty in seeing the board from certain angles. Teachers are not expected to turn into eye specialists overnight, only to become aware of some of the conditions that come within the speciality of orthoptics. A simple referral through a G.P. is all that is needed. A visit to the orthoptist is seldom a waste of time, and can provide amazing results for those for whom their remediation was necessary.

Maybe it seems a lot to ask of a busy teacher to be aware of so many matters, but it does not take much to ask every now and then if everyone can see clearly, hear distinctly, and one more question to ask: does anyone suffer discomfort or even pain when writing? If you ask a group of older pupils, you may be horrified by the proportion who say yes. It is not always so prevalent in younger ones whose pliant bodies can put up with quite a lot of distortion before they experience actual pain.

Pain is the body's warning system, it should not be ignored, or you risk developing that disturbing condition called writer's cramp when the body refuses to obey instructions to wield a pen or pencil, but will perform any other precision task.

Pain is usually the consequence of poor writing posture or strategies exacerbated when the demands for speed, and tension from other causes combine. Pupils need to be warned that pain or discomfort should not be ignored. They should feel free to complain or ask advice. Pupils should then experiment with paper positions or pen holds that allow their bodies to write (or read) in a more relaxed position.

None of these circumstances are an excuse for poor handwriting. They are just a recognition of the realities of the task. Allowances are not likely to be made in the harsh atmosphere of the outside world, and pupils have to realise that they may be judged by their handwriting even before people meet them. However, employers and others are influenced by many factors other than conventional neatness. Strength of character, originality and maturity may be equally important in many circumstances, and all these characteristics leave their mark for the experienced observer to interpret.

For pupils it should be enough to expect them to perform to their optimum rather than to some arbitrary norm, and for their teachers to be able to see when outside factors are causing excessive tension, to refrain from criticism in such circumstances and to try to uncover and remedy the cause. Handwriting need not be a series of problems. For the majority of pupils (if the vital first two years of teaching has been successful) the lightest of touches is needed. This enables handwriting to mature as the pupils themselves develop.

■ Other issues

Presentation

Marks in examinations are sometimes allotted for the general appearance and presentation of work, yet what does this word presentation mean? If you ask several schools what they mean by the word presentation, and what their policy for teaching or judging it is, you will get varying replies. Some people will shelter behind the word neatness. But neat handwriting alone will not necessarily provide a page that is easy to read. In reality, some over-neat handwriting is sometimes extremely difficult to decipher. Other schools have strict rules about such matters as margins or the underlining of titles. That will not solve the problem either.

The ability to plan a well laid out page is not a common skill, so whoever has that skill should be used in an advisory position. The newest teacher may have a better perception of layout than a much more experienced member of staff and some students may have a better concept of layout than some teachers.

Good presentation within the school includes such matters as well presented printed or written notices throughout. Such a system needs time to become effective, and a discussion of general presentation skills would help. New teachers can be introduced to the concepts, and everyone can be invited to comment on any ideas on show.

The teachers' handwriting when marking their pupils' work and elsewhere inevitably plays a part. Making sure that corrections are dealt with in a manner that does not result in covering the page with red ink shows that you value the appearance of their written work.

Here are some the issues that you need to think about.

1 You need to convey the concept that presentation is important. It can be explained that people judge you by the general appearance of your work.

2 You need to show respect for pupils' work, and also try to understand their attitudes to their own work.

3 You need to understand that presentation is a matter of considering the reader, and the way that a reader might best assimilate any particular text. It is not only concerned with the neatness of handwriting.

4 The whole school needs to consider that presentation does not have to consist of a strict list of rules.

Next you need an idea of some of the points that contribute to a well laid out page:

1 Good margins at both sides of the page.

2 Good spacing under headings and between sections.

3 Consistency of handwriting in terms of slant and proportion of letters and word spacing, rather than any particular style of handwriting.

These all contribute to ease of reading in the sense that they allow the eye to travel easily over the text. Good spacing and organisation of text assists assimilation and appreciation of a piece of writing at any age or stage. Better organisation of text comes probably more in the area of English and study skills than in handwriting or special needs. It needs to start with a discussion about how to structure an essay from the beginning.

Poor spelling and too many rubbings out invite criticism of untidiness even though inability to spell needs handling in a different way. The tensions resulting from such a problem will make writing look more uneven and jagged, even poorly spaced, as the pressures of writing are reflected in the uneven pressure of the pen on the paper.

Unrealistically slow, neat handwriting may invite praise, but instill in the writer the idea that only slow handwriting is worth anything – an inhibiting habit for a high achiever who needs speed. Even the letters written by pupils who may suffer from a condition causing a considerable tremor can be improved with good spacing and layout. These examples alone try to balance attitudes to so-called neatness. In all eventualities, neatness is a subjective matter, with some people liking one kind of neatness, while it offends another.

Some schools set out guidelines for presentation that are not always helpful. The habit of underlining titles can be ugly in the extreme if used with certain types of writing, or if the line is too close under almost any handwriting. The requirement to use capital letters for titles usually misfires too. Capital letters are seldom as well formed as small letters. When used for a title, badly written capital letters are unlikely improve the appearance of a page.

Some pupils automatically leave good spaces underneath a heading that has been written in their ordinary handwriting. This is usually effective, standing out in a pile of work that might have followed the perceived rules.

The subject of margins seems to loom large with those who like to dictate rules. Some schools state definitely that margins are permitted only on the left side. Anything else is a waste of paper. Along with that come instructions that lines should not be left between sections, and never between paragraphs. Yet some handwriting cries out for such spaces. Small, dense writing needs space for the eye to rest; and large, open writing has the same requirement, though for a different reason.

The way forward should involve more discussion and comparison and much less criticism. Teachers themselves may not be sure of how spacing relates to the size or weight of letters, and to the length of a text. A selection of pupils' work would best provide clues to what is achievable with the tools and conditions within your school. You may find that some pupils possess this innate sense of good layout that it is so difficult to define, as well as to teach.

Talking to parents

How do you talk to parents about their children's handwriting problems? What advice can or should you offer? When should you consult with other professionals? There is no easy answer to these questions. You have to deal with everything from those who think there is something wrong with their child when all is well, to those who deny that there is anything wrong when there is obviously something seriously amiss.

Starting with simple problems – parents cannot be expected to spot letterform problems. They might benefit from the relevant pages from the pupil material in this book to help them understand. Any explanation should be phrased, not as criticism, but as an explanation of how alteration is of benefit to their child – and why.

You might find dealing with matters of style to be a bit more difficult. Some parents see modern teenage handwriting as reprehensible instead of as an indication of change and perhaps practicality. Teenage peer pressure is forceful and girls in particular copy the latest fashion. Many of the signs of immaturity that infuriate some parents (such as circles on top of the letter 'i') are just that. They will disappear with a bit of growing up. Academic parents may well be dismayed if their rebellious teenager has ambitions to be a pop star and his or her writing reflects such different tastes and characteristics. Neither they nor you can alter that, but maybe you can help to defuse the situation.

It is seldom a good idea to suggest that parents should make their children practise handwriting. Indiscriminate exercises seldom solve anything. Your diagnosis and clear explanation should alert the individual to any necessary changes that need to be made. Then it is up to the individual to realise the importance of change and to practise and automate whatever needs changing in their own way. Parental nagging will certainly not help and only adds to the tension and frustration of someone struggling to retrain some aspect of written forms or writing strategy. Praise and encouragement are much more likely to succeed.

Sensitive communication within the family may be desirable. It is not, however, within your power to enforce it. If parents are not able to listen to their children's point of view by the time they are teenagers the outcome is not happy. Those pupils will have even more need of a sympathetic teacher than ever.

It is far more difficult when you suspect something is really wrong. You may suspect visual problems, for instance, but you cannot be sure. You are not a specialist so a referral to an orthoptist is the best solution. Most sensible parents would agree with your suggestion – but not all. Your suspicion may prove to be nothing, it may be something easily remedied by exercise or glasses, or occasionally it might be serious. It is not worth taking a risk.

On the whole the pupil will reveal what is the real problem – if only they are asked in a sensitive way. It is their body, so they are the experts. It is amazing and sometimes shocking what the question 'What is really bothering you?' reveals. With a physical matter it may provide the answer so that appropriate action can be taken. Be prepared for parents to be even more shocked than you when they discover that they had never noticed whatever it is that has held back their child for so long.

It is far more complex to deal with what is causing the tensions apparent in a pupil's handwriting. After careful questioning you may have discounted examinations, bullying perhaps and other school orientated issues, then only the family situation is left. What sensitive questioning in that area might reveal could be far more shocking and distressing.

How do you deal with abuse or perhaps explain to a parent that the deterioration in their child's writing is caused by their marriage breakup? A teenager may be traumatised by having had an abortion without the parents knowing anything about it – but she might blurt it out to you. Then there is a matter of confidentiality. A boy may be unsure of his sexuality and that will be reflected in his writing. (I am afraid I have seen several similar cases.) Somehow these circumstances must be faced for the sake of your pupil, but it may not always be your job. Your head teacher certainly needs to know when you cannot tell the parent, or if the parent fails to respond in an appropriate way. He or she would then be able to refer the case to a specialist if required.

Again, questioning and listening with a judicial mix of praise is the best way forward, as well as the way for everyone to understand more about these difficult problems.

Severe problems ignored or misdiagnosed

In this section I want to try and demonstrate the devastating effects of not investigating problems or misdiagnosing them. The best way of illustrating this is by relating some of the stories of children I have worked with, bearing in mind that all of such cases had been referred as handwriting problems.

This is not easy to write, nor will it be easy to read. Bear in mind that it is usually only complex problems that have been referred to me – those that no one else could sort out. I have no way of knowing how general these problems are, but even one in each school is one too many. There must be a lot of pupils but there out there suffering unnecessarily through inadequate understanding of their plight. Considering that several children sent to me had talked about suicide because of their problems, we must start to take a broader perspective. Whatever views I might hold now have been influenced by the stories that such children have related.

Teachers cannot be expected to notice and react to every aspect of those they teach, and very rarely do teachers have psychology and specialist medical expertise. What I say to primary school teachers, however, where perhaps life is more relaxed, is this: any day you might notice something different about a child which can alter that pupil's whole life. That applies equally to busy, caring secondary school teachers.

My own technique is simple, I sit children down and ask them what exactly their problem is. It is usually obvious that no one has ever treated them as intelligent enough to be asked for their opinion. The children are the experts in these situations. We need to listen and observe.

The largest proportion of problems presented to me over the years, would come under the heading of visual ones. They have ranged from pupils either missing out on school eye tests, or depending on them to have detected problems that they are not equipped to do, to serious ones needing specialist treatment, such as a suspected brain tumour.

Sometimes the answers are truly startling when children reveal that they have strange (undetected) visual or perceptual problems. One boy saw everything upside down when he tried to write. He muddled up letters like 'u' and 'n'. Another teenager, sent by a local educational psychologist, described a left to right reversal. As she put it: 'I think I see that picture as you do, but if I tried to draw it it would come out the wrong way round'. If you cannot understand that neither could I, nor anyone else that I consulted. The first pupil was learning to cope, but the second was more a intractable problem.

More wasteful of potential was the case of an older pupil, already dismissed as dyslexic and dyspraxic. He explained, when asked, that his problem was nothing to do with writing too slowly or awkwardly, only that he could not see the blackboard. He had developed strategies for note-taking so his achievements were puzzlingly variable. Poor performance at sports, not surprising as he could not see the ball, earned him the dyspraxic label. Undetected short-sightedness was his only problem and simple spectacles were all he needed. His symptoms, at the age of thirteen, could have indicated a serious sudden onset condition but his real trouble was outside my area – poor communication with parents at home and teachers at school.

An unhappy fifteen-year-old girl, in a boarding school, was supposedly a problem writer and classed as a slow learner. No investigation appeared to have been made as to the cause of her problems. You can tell so much from watching someone writing. As I sat opposite her, because, luckily there was no room to sit beside her which is my usual practice, I noticed this; her eyes did not seem to be directed where mine would have been to write. She had in fact a rather rare, but easily corrected visual problem, picked up immediately by an orthoptist.

That girl wrote an unforgettable letter which began: 'If only someone had noticed this sooner how different my life would have been.' This is understandable if you consider that at her age many pupils at that school were already sitting their external examinations while she lagged behind in almost every subject. Her appearance mirrored her unhappiness and lack of confidence.

Many conditions are misinterpreted by standard tests. One young patient presented with a psychologist's report of dyslexia, dyspraxia and poor concentration – a formidable diagnosis. It was obvious that he suffered from severe eczema. The expression on his face was tense and wary. On a hunch, I asked him whether he suffered from headaches, specifically migraine. His whole body language altered as he blurted out that his life was made a misery by headaches and their effects. He explained how he was hyperactive at the onset of an attack, clumsy and incapable of doing anything during one and too exhausted afterwards to do anything properly. 'That is when they tell me that I am not concentrating', he said. No one had ever listened to him or, as so often happens, believed a child who constantly complained of headaches. His complaints were interpreted as reluctance to go to school. He was directed to the Migraine Trust which deals with childhood as well as adult problems caused by this condition.

Another problem, better understood today than when this patient was referred (again as a handwriting problem) is severe food allergy. This child was deemed a menace as she appeared fractious and even violent at times. She disliked being touched – another clue. She was being taught in isolation which seemed extreme for a rather timid looking girl. She presented sucking a vivid orange ice lolly. As her story unfolded it became obvious that her parents had been warned about diet. They said that they were not able to be firm with four other siblings. With gentle questioning more emerged – a severe attack of measles that had necessitated a term off school, minimal brain damage perhaps, and a father who was 'severe' with her (whatever that meant) when 'she was acting up'. This was not in Great Britain and was far from any special needs assistance. My diagnosis had taken perhaps ten minutes. All I could do was to suggest a food diary which might convince them of the need to act, and give the poor child an excuse for her behaviour. She was eventually admitted to a residential unit far from home to have everything sorted out over a period of several months.

Some problems may be caused by personality clashes or misconceptions – perhaps understandable but regrettable none the less. One memorable boy had annoyed his teachers by having a handwriting that perhaps resembled the preconception of a busy doctor's script, certainly not a child's. This boy, however, was not childlike in many ways, and as a precocious student he might have been difficult to handle. He was obviously brilliant. He had an adult's mind therefore an adult's writing. His work was marked down because of this, and understandably added to his sense of injustice and frustration. To say more might make this case recognisable. It is sufficient to report that a talk with his headmaster provided a solution – no handwriting exercises needed!

There are serious health problems to consider as well. Some are obvious such as a visible disability, damaged limbs etc, but others are hidden. Some conditions require drug treatment which in turn may affect performance. I have had a stroke, so have experienced the difficulties of limbs that will not do as they are told. I have particular sympathy with those of any age who may be able to produce a passable script when writing slowly, but are chastised for not speeding up. Uncoordinated hands (legs, too) may not be able to speed up because of many marginal neurological conditions. Trying to write fast may induce confusion or even panic.

A very few people will have grown up writing with the wrong hand. Years ago that would have been attributed to teachers and parents forbidding the use of the left hand. Nowadays this is not as usual, although a child with no marked preference may still be guided towards the right hand as it is considered easiest as the world is perceived as favouring the right-handed. Now it is thought that some children are born with a weakness to what would have been their preferred one, but that side later catches up in development. In this way a pupil may have become used to using the non-preferred hand. This may cause serious problems.

One teenager gave me a lesson in the consequences. He had been referred to a therapist mainly because of behavioural problems. She suspected the cause but needed confirmation. When assured that it was so the boy's demeanour changed with relief. 'I thought that I was going mad', he said. He explained that when he wrote with the hand that he always had used there was a delay between thinking and getting that thought down on paper. When he used the other hand there was no delay between thinking and writing down. Of course, he was unpractised with the unused hand and would only be able to switch gradually as it retrained.

Relating this story to teachers in in-service talks I came across several others who had discovered that they themselves had the same problem. Recently, the sculptor Maurice Blick wrote that when he, as an adult, discovered that he had been using the wrong hand all his life it was like a filter being removed from his mind.

Writer's cramp is one more intractable and mis-understood condition. It is unlikely to occur in the early years of secondary schooling, but later on perhaps in the lead up to A Levels. Typically it is a problem of high achievers – not that handwriting problems in general are confined to less academic students. It is usually caused by poor writing strategies, often complicated with too high a perception of neatness or quality of script.

Perfectionists may be at risk if they cannot adapt their script to the speed required for note-taking and examinations. Add tension to the equation and handwriting is likely to become painful. Remember, pain is the body's warning system. If the pain becomes too severe the hand stops working properly. It cramps or makes involuntary movements.

A neurologist can ensure that nothing is seriously wrong and an occupational therapist should be able to make suggestions if the special needs teacher requires more advice. Incorrect diagnosis and treatment can be disastrous as one sixth former found out. His parents took him to a surgeon, and the resulting (unnecessary) operation made his hand so painful that it was impossible for him to sit his examinations.

Before we leave the causes of writer's cramp, you are likely as teachers, but not necessarily special needs teachers, to have in your class those who may develop trouble from an unexpected cause. It must be a relief to find work presented in a clear if somewhat immature script. However, for whatever reason, some pupils will have too high a concept of neatness. Some may have been praised or won prizes, for perfect handwriting in junior school. They never altered, keeping close to the original juvenile school model. With increasing need for speed these perfectionists are the least likely to suspect the cause of tension and even the pain as their marks fall as the result of essays that are too short.

Such writing cannot speed up sufficiently for higher education even if they manage to scrape through A Levels. People like this are typical of the writer's cramp patients I see. You are not helping these pupils by heaping praise on their neat script. It is better to teach them to scribble and in so doing develop a mature writing to fit their present and future needs.

Without underestimating any serious problems like severe dyslexia or dyspraxia, that some children may be facing, other difficulties are being exacerbated by unrealistic expectations or by being misunderstood. Some pupils are just different. Differences need not always signal deficits. We need many different skills in our society and history can provide many instances of brilliant people who were labelled underachievers at school. Yet, anyone who may only be just different, risks being labelled a problem. By being labelled a problem and treated as such, children can become real problems quite unnecessarily.

Handwriting in a multicultural context

In many classrooms today you will find pupils from other cultures who may only know the writing system that they were taught in their homeland. Although they may need to learn the rules of our writing system in the same way as five-year-olds, you are dealing with very different students. Most other writing systems are more complex than ours, with rules that have to be followed precisely. Your new pupils should pick up the basics of the letters of the alphabet, point of entry, direction and sequence of strokes, and height differentials quite easily if taught systematically in stroke related sequences.

The letters that these students usually find most difficult to write are those that look the same as in their own system but have a different movement. Many Thai characters, for instance, resemble Latin ones but are formed from the base upwards. In some Indian scripts, Tamil for instance, the round letters go clockwise making the change to an anticlockwise 'o' particularly hard. You cannot be expected to know the details of every writing system but help is at hand – ask your pupils and you will soon learn what specific aspects of letterforms they find most difficult to master.

An alteration in the direction of writing which affects Arabic, Hebrew and some other writers, might be the source of more difficulty. This is not necessarily because the writer forgets where to commence writing, but because of the differences in writing posture that may be needed to make this alteration comfortable and practical for the writer. Writing from right to left requires a different hand position from writing left to right. The wrist is often bent backwards for Arabic writers to enable them to see what they have written and to proceed quickly along the line. If they try to write that way in English it soon becomes painful. You might think it is common sense to change – but that, unfortunately, is not so. Ignoring these factors can lead to pain and frustration as the writer becomes more proficient and cannot understand why the act of writing is so uncomfortable.

Paper position may need also attention. In many cultures it is stressed that paper should be central to the writer, and not slanted. For Chinese writers this works well, as characters are detailed and there is not so much lateral movement. Written English, however, proceeds quickly from left to right, and it is preferable for the paper to be to the side of the writing hand and to slant as desired. Again this may need explaining and for the advantages to be demonstrated in a way that the writer can feel the difference.

It is true to say that we are often judged by the appearance of our handwriting. Put this into a multicultural context and it becomes more complicated. Writing in a different system is hard enough, but, in addition, your pupils are writing in a different language. Both factors will, most likely, lead to hesitancy and lack of flow in the written trace. Add to that the trauma that many will be experiencing from either voluntarily, or forcefully as refugees, leaving their homeland and their tension is likely to further distort any writing. To make any assessment taking their script into account, even of students writing in a second language alone, might be misleading. Their trace might just be indicative of other worries causing their work to appear less mature. It may not reflect their actual ability or intelligence.

With students who are learning English as a second language it can be useful to ask them to write something in their own language. You might be surprised in the difference in the standard of writing. Usually it is much more mature. Occasionally you might be able to detect something like a tremor or other fault. Then it would be realistic to expect that the same fault would be evident in their written English.

With students who are learning a new writing system, asking them to write something in their original script serves other purposes. It helps you to appreciate the complexity of their system, and enables you to observe their posture when writing. It gives you an opportunity to praise what is likely to be a more decorative writing than our own. It will add to the pupils' self esteem as you show that you value their work and it enlarges your own knowledge at the same time.

Many countries have different views on the aesthetics of handwriting. It is given a far higher priority in many countries, such as China. Even constructive criticism is best tempered with praise wherever possible when you are dealing with vulnerable pupils who may see criticism as a sign of failure.

You will probably be dealing with pupils who are keen to learn as much of the language and script as quickly as possible. The stories and poems given to young children to copy are not appropriate for your pupils. After the early stages, it is quite easy to devise exercises that combine the two skills. There will be a need to automate new letter combinations both in writing and spelling. Exercises can combine elements of language with the repetition of most common letter strings. Simple words with common word beginnings such as 'the', 'this', 'that' or 'then' followed by 'th' and other letter pairs that occur frequently at the beginning in the middle or at the end of words is a good beginning. A list of short

words that include double letters provides a different kind of repetition. Other useful sequences that can be used as exercises are:

- Comparatives and superlatives (eg tall taller tallest, fast faster fastest)
- Opposites (eg in and out, on and off, up and down. large and small)
- The different types of singulars and plurals. (eg dog dogs, class classes, potato potatoes, man men etc)
- Maybe even silent letters such as 'kn' 'hg' and 'gn' (eg know, night, and sign)

This way of combining skills and accelerating learning will motivate and benefit your pupils, at the same time making your work more interesting.

Further reading:

Sassoon R 1995 *The Acquisition of a Second Writing System.* Intellect

---

tall	taller	tallest
t............................	t............................	t............................
short	shorter	shortest
s	s	s ....
big	bigger	biggest
b	b	b ....

Part 2

So you are having trouble with your handwriting

As the teacher you might think that this first page is inappropriate but it has a particular purpose. Whatever you say about pupils' work may be construed as criticism of their handwriting. Teenagers' handwriting, or anyone else's for that matter, for better or worse, is part of themselves. They may react strongly to it being criticised even though it is for their own good. It is important to break through the 'them and us' situation as quickly as possible.

It is only natural for a pupil to think 'I can read it why can't they'. To be fair, sometimes pupils cannot even decipher the teacher's message. What I am trying to do here is to put you in their place, to understand what they need to have explained and what preconceptions you may have to overcome.

The remarks below, made by various teachers are not exactly helpful. They do not explain what is needed and seem only to be expressing their own exasperation. This is understandable when faced with an illegible script. You must, however, be on the pupils' side, and somehow communicate that the trouble with their writing, whatever it is, is unlikely to be their fault, Either they have not been taught properly or there is something really wrong. They cannot diagnose their own problems, so it is your role to discover, with their help, what can be done.

So you are having trouble with your handwriting

You can read it, why can't they?

Do people keep saying that they cannot read what you have written? Other people judge you by your writing but they look for individuality as well as neatness. Good writing must of course be legible but it should flow and have some character.

You do not need the same standard of handwriting all the time. It must be extra good if you are writing a special letter, but when you are writing a quick list for yourself it can be really rough. For note-taking and examinations speed is the most important thing and for this you need an in-between standard.

Handwriting is for communicating, not only while you are at school, but for the rest of your life. If there are any real problems it is worth getting things right now.

This is how you can start

No one can force pupils to change anything about their handwriting. It must all come from them in the end. What you are going to try to alter are actual movements of the body – movements that have long been automated. You are also going to alter attitudes which may also be deeply ingrained and you have no idea who or what influenced the writer in the habits or tensions that are now showing.

The questions below are a good start. They focus the writers' attention on their own habits and problems in a non-confrontational way. You can discuss any or all of the points with the pupil. In this way you will both start with a better understanding of the issues involved – and of each other.

The collection of pens is a reminder of one of the best relaxing techniques for you to use. Collect as wide a variety of writing implements as possible. These will include different types of points and different widths, from the familiar biros to fibre tips and gel pens. This gives a choice of the many free flowing pen points. Then you need a wide variety of handles – thick ones, thin ones, long ones, short ones and unusual angled ones like the new Yoropen. Let the pupils try them, perhaps just writing their name with each one. They can then choose to write with the one they find most comfortable and suited to their script. Occasionally this will, in itself, provide a solution to their problem. It is always an interesting exercise and usually shows how the writing will improve as the writer relaxes into an enjoyable and probably unexpected exercise.

This is how you can start

Some so-called handwriting problems have little to do with the letters themselves. Your attitude to your handwriting, the way you use your body, and any other problems with your school work will also affect how you write

It is simplest to consider your letters first. If someone explains what might be wrong with the way your letters are formed you may be able to deal with that by yourself. There are pages like this one called 'Spot your own mistakes'. Some of you may find them useful. You yourself must be convinced that change is necessary, and want to make the appropriate alterations. It is up to you in the end.

Handwriting needs to be automatic to leave your mind free to think about other things. You want to concentrate on what you are writing, not what your hand is doing. To get to this level you need proper training. If you've missed out earlier on, this gives you another chance. Half the problem is understanding what is wrong. Putting it right may be easier than you think.

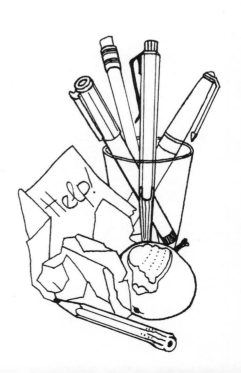

First, ask yourself these questions:

Is my handwriting worse under pressure?

Does it hurt to write?

Is it so slow that I never get enough done?

Is it so fast that it looks sloppy?

Is it just *my* writing that is bad? What about other people's?

Is it worth all the effort to improve things?

Ask yourself these questions again when you have dealt with your problems.

Before you even start to write

This page again focuses the writers' attention on how they write. Before suggesting solutions this offers a list of questions for pupils to ask themselves. It sets the scene for you to offer help – but be sure that your advice is really helpful. Read the pages 22 and 23 concerning observation first so that you have an understanding of the issues involved. Your attitude must always be concerned with what benefits the writer. There is no exact right or wrong about any aspect of handwriting. Anything of concern, or disagreement for that matter, can be settled through discussion.

This is the time to consider any unusual postures and if appropriate to question (very sensitively) to try and find out if this might be a cause for an atypical posture or paper position. Observation of a variety of pupils will begin to give you a feeling for the different causes. Maybe no one has ever suggested a change of paper position to them, or asked them whether they have an aching hand or back. This is also an ideal moment to investigate other issues such as whether a pupil can see the board from every position in the classroom – or check that he or she can hear the teacher. Although these issues are outside handwriting problems they are at the very centre of consideration for the pupil.

Occasionally, a pupil will not enjoy, or may not be willing to see the relevance of, this stage of questioning. In this case change to the letterform aspect on page 36 onwards and come back to these pages later on.

Before you even start to write

It really helps if:

1   You can see what you are doing.

2   Your desk is the right height for you.

3   Your desk has a good surface.

4   Your paper is in the best position for you.

5   Your pen suits both your hand and your writing.

6   You hold your pen in a way that lets your fingers move freely.

7   You try to keep your desk clear and tidy.

Chair too low. Shoulders hunched. Hand twists so you can see to write.

Two cushions. Comfortable height. Hand straightens. Writing can flow.

Correct desk height. Arms supported. Shoulders relaxed. Writing improves.

What to do about it and why

It is quite likely that you will have little influence on what happens in general classrooms. such as specifying the size of furniture or the lighting in any particular room. You can, however, help to ensure that the individual pupils that you are helping as a special needs teacher, or whole class that you may be addressing, know the optimum conditions for working. In the end the onus will have be on them to influence their own working conditions in school and in their working lives.

If you are working with individuals you may be able to demonstrate how alterations in quite simple things can make a big difference to the standard and comfort of writing. You could arrange to fit the chair and desk height to individuals. Then at least they will experience the effects of an optimum position. Even in countries that supply adjustable desks, these are of minimal use in schools where pupils are constantly changing classrooms – individually that is a different matter.

Rough work tops, of the type that are often found in science labs, can cause havoc with handwriting. To solve this problem, place a pad of paper under the writing sheet. This is also effective when working on hard shiny surfaces. At the same time give pupils the opportunity to write on a slanting surface. Special writing slopes are available commercially and should be in every special needs unit. It is quite easy for individuals to make use of something unobtrusive once they experience the benefit of support for the whole arm. A ring binder with the fat part away from the body gives quite a bit of support. Pen hold and paper position are dealt with in detail between pages 26 and 31.

What to do about it and why

1   If you are right-handed, try to have the light coming from the left. If you are left-handed have the light coming from your right or you'll be working in the shadow of your hand.

2   Make sure that you sit comfortably. If your chair is too low you will be hunched up, with your chin almost on the desk. If your chair is too high or the table is too low, then you may end up sitting sideways because there is no room for your legs.

3   Rough dents leave dents in the paper and make your writing jerky. Plastic desks are often too hard. Write on a pad of paper or rest on something that will give slightly.

4   If you are right-handed, your paper should always be to your right side. If you are left-handed it should be over to your left. This lets your arms move freely as you write and stops you twisting your wrist to see what you are writing. Once the paper is over to the correct side you can slant it to suit yourself.

5   Experiment with different types of pens to find out how they affect your writing and your comfort.

6   Ask to see the pages 26 to 30 for information about pen hold.

7   If there is too much junk piled up on your desk, you may find yourself twisted over to one side because that is the only flat space for your paper. Remember, a right-hander will need space to the right and a left-hander to the left.

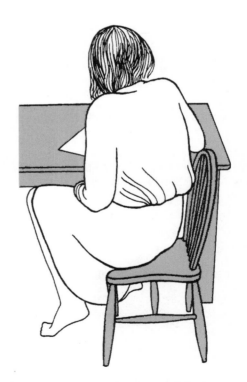

This table is too low and the chair too small.
Sitting sideways is bad for handwriting.

If you do not believe all this, do the opposite. See how it feels and what it does to your writing.

Pen holds

Pen holds are one of the most emotive and least understood issues in the classroom as well as in the home. Writers are unfairly criticised and pen holds blamed for poor handwriting, but the blame lies elsewhere. All was well when everyone used conventional pencils and pens. At least everyone knew approximately the best way to hold them. The trouble started with the advent of ballpoints and other kinds of modern pens. They are practical and a vital part of modern life, but no one seemed to anticipate the trouble that would be caused by their having to be held at different elevations in order to work properly. They do not perform at the low slant that a pencil did. The most usual way to get them upright is either to exert more pressure on one side with one or two fingers, or for the thumb to push harder. This usually results in forcing it to slide further across the handle.

Unconventional holds start early as most infants use felt tipped pens before they come to school, seldom coloured pencils. As the felt tips get worn they have to be held in an ever more upright position. The muscles adapt easily at this early stage and the child becomes accustomed to whichever method works well. Afterwards it becomes increasingly hard to alter – and often seems unnecessary. The best way for you, the teacher, to understand, is to try these slight alterations in the finger positions yourself and experience the differences they make. The harder you press the more the pen comes upright.

The three questions that are posed here are important because the motivation to alter an unconventional pen hold must come from the writer. Discuss them first.

Pen holds

The way you hold your pen affects your handwriting more than you realise. It can make the difference between an aching hand and trouble-free writing. Ask yourself these questions.

1   Does it hurt me to write for any length of time?

2   Can I write as fast as I want to?

3   Does the way I hold my pen distort my letters or restrict my movements?

If the answer to any of these is 'yes', then read on.

The conventional way of holding a pen is called a tripod grip. You put your thumb and first finger gently on either side of the pen and your middle finger underneath. This way everything can move freely as you write. If you have a problem you must look at each part of your grip separately: your finger position, your hand position and your wrist.
Let us start with the fingers.

Try these different finger positions.

It even makes a difference which finger is nearest the pen point. When the first finger is in front you can make the quick changes of direction that you need in writing. When the thumb is in front you have less control over the pen. You may end up with an awkward handwriting, or a nasty lump where the pen is pressed down on your middle finger. As your thumb goes forward your first finger gets forced up at a sharp angle. This can be painful.

Forefinger in front.

Thumb and finger equal.

Thumb in front.

Hand positions

It is not only the fingers that influence the pen hold and consequent writing but the position of the hand (the rotation of the wrist). The two positions illustrated below both work well. Many artistic people adopt the on edge hand position automatically. This position produces a forward slant to written letters whereas a slightly flattened hand results in a more upright script. Try it yourself.

It is only when the wrist becomes excessively on edge so that it twists the hand that it may become painful. This tends to occur when left-handers find that they cannot see what they have written. The solution then is to move the paper further over to the writer's left. This does not automatically solve the trouble when some writers may have with altering their hand position. They may have become so used to it. The best motivation for change comes when writing becomes painful. Some left-handers also alter spontaneously when they find that when their wrist is twisted so their hand comes from above the line they cannot speed up their writing.

Discuss all these ideas and show the illustrations on pages 28-29. Also try to replicate some of your pupils' pen holds. In this way you will understand that you would find it hard to alter the way you hold your pen just as they do,

---

Hand positions

Do you write with your hand on edge, or is it slightly flattened? The 'hand on edge' way works well if you are relaxed but can cause trouble if you are tense. Under pressure you can tip your hand too far over so your wrist twists. This can hurt. Flatten your hand a little, so that your wrist straightens automatically. This soon stops the pain. Do not go to the other extreme and flatten your hand too much or you will make another set of muscles ache.

The tripod grip works well with a pencil or a fountain pen but not always so well with modern pens. They have to be held more upright to work well. This may be why so many people have unconventional pen holds. Some work quite well. There is an alternative pen hold that helps to cure pain and writer's cramp. Ask to see the illustration (no 7) on page 29. If your pen hold is causing you trouble you must do something about it. First find which part of your hand or arm is strained. Experiment with different positions until your whole hand can relax and move freely.

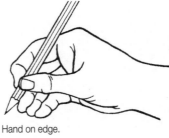

Hand on edge.

Hand slightly flattened.

It may take a while to get your muscles used to a new writing position. Start with some of the relaxing scribbles on page 33 before you try long sentences.

When you alter your hand or finger position the slant or proportions of your writing can change. Alternatively if you want to change the slant of your writing play around with your hand position or pen hold.

Unconventional pen holds – left hand

All these drawings were taken from actual photographs and give an idea of some of the different strategies that people adopt. Some work quite well but others do not. The result of no 1 can be seen on page 31. This boy could manage quite well at primary school and saw no reason to alter. Later on his attempts at fast writing invited so much criticism as well as intense pain in his hand and neck that he agreed to change his paper position and try a different hand position and pen hold. He never looked back. No 2 has a twisted wrist (inverted position) and two fingers on the handle of the pen. These factors combined are not too helpful but maybe the two finger hold is an indication of long fingers, which in themselves can cause problems. No 3 is also slightly inverted but obviously relaxed, and probably adopted this position to allow his writing to slant forwards. Over goes the thumb, but it is allowing the pen to be upright. No 4 shown on page 30 allowed so little free movement that it resulted in a small, restricted script. It can work but often is slow and can be painful. No 5, with the thumb right over the handle, would result in less control over fine movements but the writer would not have much motivation to change. No 6 looks complicated but might well work quite well for the writer,

Notice that most of the left-handers' pens slant in a different direction to the right-handers. That in turn will affect the slant of their handwriting. It is difficult for left-handers to have forward slanting script.

Unconventional pen holds – left hand

Left-handers try to solve their special problems, but do not always succeed.

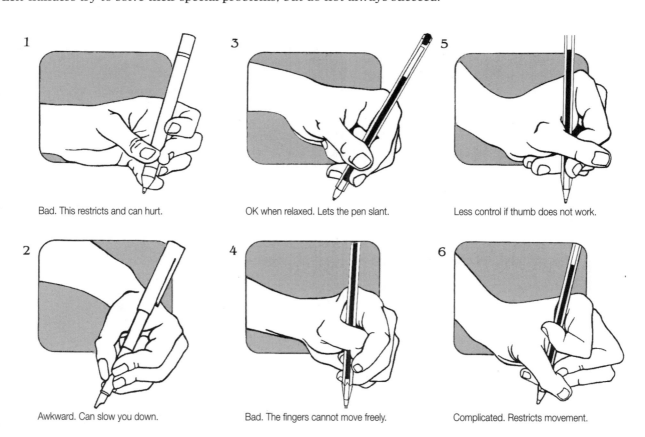

1 Bad. This restricts and can hurt.

2 Awkward. Can slow you down.

3 OK when relaxed. Lets the pen slant.

4 Bad. The fingers cannot move freely.

5 Less control if thumb does not work.

6 Complicated. Restricts movement.

Unconventional pen holds – right hand

No 7 may look unconventional but is an excellent pen hold. The pen is held between the index and middle finger so there is never the pressure that causes a callous and pain. By freeing the fingers it lets writing flow more easily. It should be recommended for anyone who is suffering from pain or tension, but it is disliked by those who are very conventional. It is also useful for those with long fingers. See example No 8. It may appear conventional but the angle of finger and thumb indicate a tense and painful pen hold, therefore probably a tense writer as well. No 9 has two fingers on the pen but this time the fingers are not synchronised. This may be caused by long fingers but may be slowing the writer down. It would probably be difficult to alter. No 10 looks complicated but may work quite well so beware of criticising it. Observe how the thumb of no 11 is pushing the pen. This will not work well but the writer, I suspect, would be unwilling to alter unless, or more likely, until, it hurts her. No 12 is an example of what you can learn. When questioned as to why she had adopted this complex pen hold (a useful technique), this girl looked at her hand in amazement. She exclaimed that she started holding the pen that way when she broke her finger and could not think why she was still doing it – but she had got used to it and it worked well.

So, observe and question and maybe help the writer to find something more effective – but only if necessary. By now you will be realising that possibly the pupils will be no more likely to be able to hold their pen like you do, than you are likely to hold yours like they do theirs.

Unconventional pen holds – right hand

You need to try out these pen holds to feel why some work and others do not

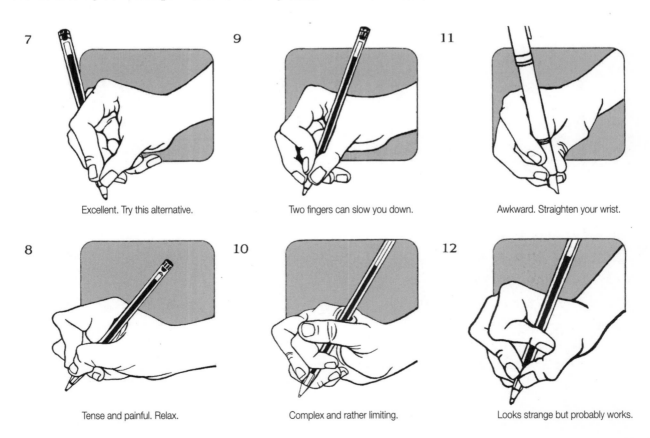

| 7 Excellent. Try this alternative. | 9 Two fingers can slow you down. | 11 Awkward. Straighten your wrist. |
| 8 Tense and painful. Relax. | 10 Complex and rather limiting. | 12 Looks strange but probably works. |

Your hand and your handwriting

The way you hold your pen affects your writing for better or worse. In many cases there is neither the need nor desire to change, but these few illustrations help to show when intervention might succeed. The first writer, an art student, was dismayed by her immature script. Much of her difficulty was caused by her long fingers. In order to fit onto the pen she had a stiff two finger pen hold. Long fingers can often be the cause pain when writing. The second picture shows how changing to the alternative pen hold had immediate effect. Her fingers could relax and straighten out and her writing altered to a free flowing, forward slanting script – all in five minutes. It is not always so easy!

The other writer shown below did not come to me for advice – I sat opposite to this university student on a train and asked to take a picture of her pen hold. I doubt whether she would have taken kindly to change. Pen hold, like every other aspect of handwriting, is an indicator. Looking at her bitten nails and this extremely tense hold adopted to give maximum control, she gave the impression of a tense and insecure person. This pen hold, at least, succeeded in getting the ballpoint upright but the effect on the handwriting was only too obvious. The limited movement allowed by the way the pen was held made the script almost indecipherable. If attempted, the alternative pen hold usually works well for left-handers and allows a clear line of sight to the written words. Not all writers will be willing to experiment with it and I suspect that this writer would be one of those who would refuse.

Your hand and your handwriting

The way you hold your pen affects your letterforms. Your whole hand as well as your fingers need to move freely to produce all the different strokes. Your pen hold should be relaxed to let you write fast and painlessly. Change pen hold, for whatever reason and you will probably alter the shape and slant of your letters.

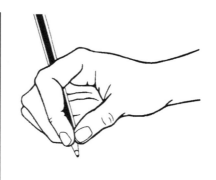

This is a tense pen hold. The hand is on edge with two fingers stiffly on the pen. The hand cannot move freely enough to make joining strokes. A slow, rather childish printing is the result. Write like this for long and it will hurt.

A complete change of pen hold gave immediate relief. The hand is slightly flattened, the fingers relaxed, and the writing now flows. This unconventional but efficient pen hold is specially good for those with long fingers.

This pen hold is bad. It does not let the fingers move. The limited movement shows in the writing. The hand pushes along the line but cannot go up and down, so there is hardly any difference between the tall and short strokes.

Paper position affects how you sit and what you write

If you only had the written sample to look at it would be difficult to work out what had caused the strung out handwriting in the first example below. That is why it is so important to see the writer in action. It is also an example of how difficult it is to self diagnose, or surely this boy would have realised what was wrong. To any one watching it is obvious that his paper is in the wrong position and needs moving. He is right-handed and the paper is way out to his left so he had to move his hand over in order to see the next letter. In doing so he kept the pen on the paper. A change of paper position solved those extended top joins.

The central pen hold was illustrated on page 28 but here it is shown with the boy's handwriting. No wonder he faced criticism. This sample was once shown to an eminent psychologist who announced that the writer suffered from a severe neurological complaint. Without seeing the writer in action a diagnosis can be quite wrong. His whole posture is not illustrated, but the strain of twisting his head to try and see what he was writing was causing severe headaches, A change of paper position allowed his hand to untwist, and a short time later he was unable to return to the painful position that was wrecking his comfort and his work – hence a 'before' but no 'after' illustration.

As a right-hander in the last illustration, there is no obvious reason for the inverted (twisted) hand position. Look at what it is doing to the boy's thumb. In this case he was having to follow an italic model which did not suit him, Maybe this was the reason. He would not consider altering the way he was writing. At times like this all you can do is to make suggestions and hope that when or if he starts to experience pain he will remember what you said and do something about it.

Paper position affects how you sit and what you write

Where you place the paper is vital. It influences how you sit, hold the pen and, in the end, what you write. Alter the paper position if it makes you sit awkwardly – left-handers more to their left and right-handers to their right. Arm muscles and even those in your back are used in writing. They must learn to work together in a new position. It may feel odd at first.

The paper is over the wrong side. The writer sits badly and cannot see what he is doing. Letters, specially those that join at the top, spread out as he pulls his hand across to make sure he has written the right thing.

Some strokes are almost impossible to form with this pen hold. Change it or you will have awkward writing. Left-handers need the paper over to the left so they do not have to twist the wrist to see what they are doing.

Some right-handers also twist the wrist and push with the thumb. Once again the result is awkward, jerky writing and an aching hand. Correct paper position will avoid this unnecessary trouble.

Relax and your handwriting will improve

This is one of the most intractable, yet commonest problems that you have to deal with. Tension is the greatest distorter of handwriting. The typical uneven or jagged script often appears unsightly but signals a need for understanding not criticism. You may suspect the source of the tension, whether at school or at home, but you have little control over it. In some cases it may not even be advisable to investigate that aspect too deeply. In others the pupil will be desperately in need of a sympathetic teacher to help them out of some trouble – and you may well be shocked by some of their revelations.

You will soon recognise the signs of tension. Then by some means you need to get the person in front of you gradually to relax. In that way both of you will soon be able to see the subtle changes in handwriting. The exercise suggested on page 23 which involves choosing a pen and name writing is useful in these circumstances. Look at the hunched shoulders pictured below. They all seem to suggest tension. If you walk behind your pupils' chairs you will get another view of those who need to relax.

None of this solves the causes of tension. What it does do is to show the writer that when he or she relaxes many of the visible problems disappear. At least pupils then have proof that when they are happy and in a relaxed environment their handwriting is acceptable. You have little influence over what happens in other situations and may feel it advisable to tell pupils that their writing may again deteriorate under stress.

✂ --

Relax and your handwriting will improve

There is tension in all our lives, at home and at school. When the stress gets really bad, this will show in your writing. Then you may be criticised for bad writing or untidiness. You may grip your pen so hard that it hurts you to write. You may be pressing too hard on the paper so that your letters go through several sheets. Your hand can look quite relaxed, but tension can be stiffening your arm or shoulder. The way you sit can make your muscles tense, or tension itself can make you sit awkwardly. You may sometimes be so worried, angry or frustrated that neither your thoughts nor your writing can flow freely. It is all connected.

You cannot get rid of all the worry and tension in your life, but you can learn to relax when writing.

1   Sit with your back straight. Relax your hand and arm.

2   Uncross your legs. Relax your hunched shoulders.

3   Shake your hand until it feels floppy. Take a couple of deep breaths.

Stiff neck and shoulders are the result if you sit badly. These three all need to move the paper – left-handers to their left, right-handers to the right, to relax.

Relaxing scribbles

These relaxing scribbles mimic the movement of handwriting. They take away any problems of producing actual letters and allow the writer to feel how smooth the act of writing could feel. These scribbles are useful when writers are testing a different pen or an altered pen hold that might feel too unfamiliar. It could put them off at first, but the scribbles are an ideal way of getting used to something new.

If a pupil's problem manifests itself through too much pressure on the page, then you can turn over the paper and feel a lessening of the indentations on the back as the writer relaxes. As you can see the three scribbles get progressively more controlled. The bottom one provides a quick but very useful glimpse into your pupil's character and possible difficulties. This is illustrated on page 72.

Relaxing scribbles

Try these relaxing scribbles. They make you loosen up and realise that you can write this way all the time. You can learn a lot about your writing problems by looking closely at your own efforts. Do them until your pen is skimming across the page. This how it should feel when you are writing.

Can you do both the rounded movements and the joining strokes between the long and short lines? Do you hesitate anywhere? If so try changing your pen hold to help your fingers move more freely.
Do you feel that your pen is holding you up, perhaps not moving as smoothly as it ought? If so, it is time you used a more flowing point. What about trying a fibre-tip or gel pen?
When you started did you press so hard that you could feel the bumpy shapes through the back of the paper? If so, you are using too much force. You do not need to keep turning over the paper to check whether you are improving as you relax. As you put less pressure on the pen the lines get fainter.

Practical tips for left-handers

It might help you to understand the practical problems if you try to write with your left hand (presuming you are right-handed). The effects will be pretty wild but at least you will have a better understanding of the practical difficulties. Sometimes the only thing you can do is to set up the optimum conditions for individuals to let them feel and see if it suits them better. The sad truth is that it is still a right-handed world and with handwriting, like so many things, they may have to find their own ways of surviving. The list below can only alert them to some of the issues involved. Discuss these issues as well, and between you, you might come up with some useful suggestions for the whole school.

A few left-handers write with their left hand but have a right leading eye. That is described as being cross lateral. Their paper position will have to be a compromise between the needs of hand and the eye. The more complex problems of directionality and difficulties with specific letters and joins are explained on pages 9-10 and page 47.

The Yoropen's angle helps left-handers because it allows them to see what they have just written.

Practical tips for left-handers

Left-handers have different needs from right-handers and these are often overlooked.

1 Sit at the end of the table, or next to a left-hander. You need space to your left side. If you sit to the right of a right-hander, you will bump each other as you work.

2 Find a seat where the strong light comes from your right side, otherwise you will be working in the shade of your own hand.

3 Sit a little higher than your right-handed neighbour. This will help you to see over the top of your hand as you write. Hold your pen a fair distance from the point to help you to see what you are writing.

4 Paper position is very important. Put the paper to your left side before you start to slant it. Your arm can move freely. You see what you are doing without smudging.

5 A pen with a smooth point will work best for you. Sharp points dig into the paper and broad edged nibs can be a problem. Fibre tips are good and do not smudge.

6 Some strokes are more difficult for a left-hander. You may want to use slightly different letters from a right-hander, or sequence your strokes differently. See page 47.

This left-hander had his paper over to his right side, so he sat sideways to write.

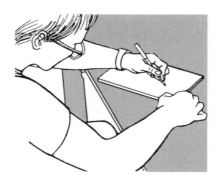

Now the paper is in the over to his left he can sit properly at the desk.

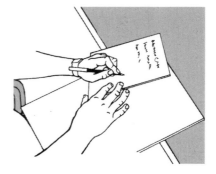

He tried working on a tilted board and liked it too. You might like it too.

Hand positions for left-handers

The strategies that some pupils have adopted may appear strange and uncomfortable to you but may work quite well for individuals. Questioning may reveal why that particular posture has been adopted. This may add to your understanding but as far as intervention goes the same rules apply as on page..

Does it hurt? Does it slow down the writer? Is it distorting any letters or strokes?

Like everything else about handwriting hand postures can form early in school life, quite unconsciously. They are influenced by various factors, paper position being perhaps the most important. If children have enough space and are helped to place their paper to their left then maybe all will be well. If not they develop their hand position around their paper, such as twisting their wrist above the line of writing. The way they slant the paper as the arm gets longer and needs more space may result, sometimes quite markedly, in writing upwards or downwards on the paper.

This illustration shows that the angle of the paper determines whether you write upwards or downwards

Hand positions for left-handers

When it comes to holding a pen, there seem to be three main hand positions that left-handers choose.

1   Over the top sometimes called inverted. The wrist is twisted right round so that the pen comes down from above the line of letters. If you want to change from this position first move the paper over to your left then flatten your hand slightly. Your wrist then straightens.

This hand is twisted so the pen comes from above the line of writing.

Advantages

You can see what you are doing. You do not smudge your work. You can make your letters slant forward easily.

Disadvantages

It is awkward and can hurt you. It may slow your writing down. It is difficult to make an undercurve or joining stroke.

2   From the side. Provided you make your fingers work and do not push the pen with your whole hand, this can be an effective way to write. Notice the way the paper can slant.

This hand comes in from the side

Advantages

You can see what you have just written. You do not smudge. Letters are usually upright.

3   From below. Provided you slant your paper and have it well to your left, you should see what you have just written.

This hand comes from below the writing.

Advantages

Your fingers probably move more freely with less pushing. It is easier to join up and lets the writing flow. You are less likely to be criticised.

Disadvantages

Your writing may slope backwards.

Handwriting is a pattern

The fact that handwriting is a pattern is greatly to everyone's advantage when it comes to teaching in the first place or correcting later on. Pay no attention to people who say that you cannot change the way pupils form their letters when they get to secondary school. You cannot force anyone to alter any of their letters that have the wrong movement, but you can persuade them that it is to their benefit. That is done by demonstrating that by getting the movement right their hand will move more smoothly, that letters can then join and it will be quicker and more efficient.

Pupils must be able to feel this as well as see this. The easiest way is by using a pattern of letters from the same family as the faulty one

For instance for the frequently wrongly formed 'd' try: cd cd cd

For 'a' or 'g' try ca ca ca for 'g' try cg cg cg then adadad which is a bit harder

For 'n', 'm', and 'r' when they are written without the first stroke:

hnhnhn hmhmhm hrhrhr progressing to nrnrnr and mrmrmr

Try it first in separate letters before embarking on joined up then words using the same family of letters. You can apply the same principle to any letters finding a suitable partner with the same movement within the same family. See also the opposite page.

Handwriting is a pattern

Think of written letters as a pattern made up of very few strokes. There are long and short straight strokes, diagonal ones and rounded ones. That leaves only dots and crosses on the letters 'i', 'j', 'f' and 't'.

Putting letters in family groups:

You can separate letters into those using the same strokes and deal with them in family groups. But remember it is meant to be a moving pattern.
It is important to start at the right place and write the strokes in the correct direction. Then when the letters join up they make an understandable pattern.

i l t j   are made up of straight strokes.

u y   have under arches.

h n m r b p k   have a downstroke followed by an arch.

c a d g q o e   are all based on 'c' even though 'e' starts further round.

v w x z   have diagonal strokes and so does this 'k'.

f s   start like 'c' then change direction.

All letters start at the top except 'e' and 'd'. This is a useful tip.

If the pattern is wrong ...

It is not only that letters with an incorrect movement make joined letters almost impossible to read but they often stop the writer from joining up at all. In the script below the only letter that joins is the incorrectly formed 'd', If you wanted to impress on pupils how inefficiently the hand would move in this case, enlarge the sample and let them trace it with their own hand. By replicating the movement they will be able to feel how jerky and odd it feels. It takes the sting out of correcting their own writing and brings home the message without any tension.

If you were going to correct this boy (or any other pupil) you could start by looking for a letter with the correct movement. In this case the 'a' and the 'g' work well, so you could say that at least he has got two of the most difficult letters right and then go on to the rest of that family and deal with the 'd' and the 'o' which appears to go round the wrong way, He needs almost every pattern exercise:

bh bh bh and probably bhp bhp bhp even though 'p' does not appear in this sample.

His 'y' looks all right so yu yu yu will help and of course hmn hmn hmn

It would be a long job and it is hard to understand how this problem could have been left so long. It may come down to this feeling that you cannot change the letters of older pupils. This is just not true and you must try. You are probably the pupil's last chance.

✂

If the pattern is wrong ...

Wrongly formed letters can make joined up writing almost impossible to read. A smoothly flowing movement leads to a more efficient handwriting and is less strain on your hand.

a young man Fi'nd ovt about murder and under

Many of these letters are wrongly formed. They must be corrected before they can join properly.

1	Starting at the wrong place		2	Going round the wrong way	
↑O	leads to 𝛼𝛼 instead of OO		O↘	leads to 𝜕𝜕 instead of OO
d↓	leads to ded instead of ded		𝔊	leads to gro instead of go

3	Leaving strokes out		4	Adding strokes on	
↑m	leads to hum instead of him		ui	leads to uiin instead of win
↑r	leads to art instead of art		u	leads to eue instead of eve

Check the points on these pages against your own writing or get a couple of friends to do it for you.

Alternatives and other families

Handwriting models differ even within this country and with a mobile population you will be faced with a variety of letterforms. It is not a good idea to make pupils change from the style that they have been taught. Should they, however, have movement problems that need correcting just bear in mind that some letters may have to move into another family so will need a different letter to partner them.

For those who have problems with the heights of letters it may be enough for them to have the alphabet demonstrated in the groups shown below. In addition they will benefit from an explanation as to why the height differentials are so important. The different heights define the shape of the word. Their handwriting may be just about legible while slow and deliberate but when they have to speed up the conventional ascenders and descenders are vital. If they need further help then exercises will mean writing first the separate groups – best on lined paper – then words with mixed heights.

Alternatives and other families

You may have learned other forms of certain letters. If so, your groups might be different.

ʊ and ʊ would go with u y Rounded ʊ and w might go with them.

You can use these letter groups to make your own exercises.

How to make up your own exercises:

If you have a faulty letter just find another in the same family that you can write correctly. Repeat them together a few times. The right one will help the wrong one to move correctly.

Grouping letters by height:

b d f h k l   go above the line of writing.

f g j p q y   go below the line of writing.

a c e i m n o r s u v w x z   do not go up or down.

t   is taller than 'i' but not as tall as 'l'.

t f   are a useful pair if you are having crossbar troubles.

If you are having trouble with heights of letters use these groups for your exercise.

If the letter heights are wrong ...

These samples illustrate typical faults in various styles. When you are writing out exercises for a pupil it is a good idea to keep approximately to their style and slant. As you can see each style seems to encourage different faults. The first one seems to be joining up before he has got the right idea about the different heights of letters. The exercises for this pupil will need to be in separate letters before he goes back to joins – and even then it might be better if he did not join from ascending letters.

The next sample illustrates the particular faults that might arise from a style with this 'f', 'b' and open 'p'. The sample that slopes backwards came from a left-hander. It illustrates that as 'f' is the only letter that can both ascend and descend. If written as a long letter it can be simplified to a straight line with a crossbar.

Twelve rules of legibility

As handwriting matures and speed forces some modifications, letters need no longer be written absolutely perfectly. Words like 'must look' and 'be indicated' are used rather than 'must be' or 'must appear' over the page. These words reflect the realities of mature scripts. The twelve rules illustrated on page 40 are showing what liberties you can take and get away with, and what you cannot – and what happens when you go too far.

If the letter heights are wrong ...

Make letters the right height or your writing will be difficult to read.

This says 'hill will' and 'here were'. The short 'h' and bad joins from the 'w' muddle the words.

These sequences help to correct the letter heights

Here the letters that should go below the line cause the trouble.

This says 'be fit for a bit of painting' but the letter 'f' is too short and can get confused with the open 'b'. The open 'p' is too short. It looks like a letter 'n'.

You can simplify the letter 'f' but it must go below the line or it looks like a 't'. See the short 'h'.

'f' and 'l' are too short. A stroke left off the 'u' in 'grateful' makes matters worse.

12 rules of legibility

These points apply to separate letters as well as joined up letters:

1 Letters must be the correct height in relation to each other.

after class not *after class*

2 Letters meant to be closed must look closed.

ing an not *ing an*

3 Letters that are meant to be open must look open.

hay out not *bay out*

4 Straight strokes must look straight.

all living not *all living*

bit is not *bit is*

5 Curved strokes must look curved.

ice not *ice*

6 Parts of letters meant to be joined together must be joined.

backs not *backs*

pack not *pack*

7 Loops and arches must appear, also crossbars and dots on 'i'.

The who not *The who*

8 Overcurves and undercurves must differ.

hum not *hum*

or *hum*

9 Space letters so that it is clear where one letter ends and the next begins.

aging bat not *aging bat*

These points apply to joined up letters:

10 Finish one letter before starting the next.

was we not *was we*

11 The joining stroke must be indicated or space left to show where one letter ends and the next begins.

her lain not *her hair*

12 The joining must not distort a letter so that it looks like another, or suggest an extra letter.

give way not *give way*

Why and when to join up

Recently the fashion has been to encourage children in junior schools to join up every letter in every word. However, as ever longer words get used all that happens is that letters can become distorted and hands can begin to ache. This is because we have to rest the whole of our hand on the writing surface in order to control modern implements. We need to take pen lifts during long words. In the days when quills were used and continuous copperplate was written, the hand was balanced precariously on the little finger only. Joining up is only going from where you finish one letter to where you start the next. When you lift the pen exactly the same movement takes place in the air instead of on the paper, therefore it wastes little time or energy.

The phrase 'join when comfortable' is important. You may find just as many problems with pupils who join too much as with those who do not join enough. Often the trouble is evident when less competent writers join from descenders. These strokes tend to distort the pattern of the writing.

The reasons listed here are useful for discussion. What is not mentioned is that pupils with severe problems may feel safer with separate letters until their other difficulties are sorted out. There is always the other side of the argument. For some conditions, children with tremors for instance, it is repositioning that is difficult. Within reason, they will find joined up works better for them.

Why and when to join up

Reasons for joining once you're used to it:

1   It is usually faster.
2   It is more mature.
3   It helps the flow of writing and this also makes it easier for your hand.
4   It spaces your writing as well as joining it.

Reasons against joining if you are not used to it:

1   Sometimes it is less legible.
2   At first it may not be so neat.
3   It may be slower until you have practised.

You do not need to join all your letters all the time. Your hand needs a rest, and a chance to move along the line too. Continuous joining of long words makes writing slower, not quicker. Start with the joins that come easiest to you and join when it is comfortable.

Simple joins have groups too

Letters that can join from the base   i l t u h m n a d c e k

Letters that can join from the top   o r v w

Letters that can join from the crossbar   f t

Letters that can join with loops at speed   f g j y q

Letters that are joined over the top and back   a c d e g o q

Letters that you can join or leave unjoined   b p s x z

Start joining in easy stages

It is often necessary to overcome pupils' fear that joining is difficult. There are tricks to overcome this and to let them feel at once the sensation of skimming along with simple joins. One way to do it is to start with the pattern of joined long and short strokes. Then change to one short and two long and there is the word 'ill'. Then progress to hill, hilly, etc. gradually building up to longer words with the simplest joins. It is rather cheating as you know that there are difficulties ahead with more complex combinations – but it is a start.

It is necessary that pupils should eventually know how to join every letter to every other – but in pairs or short words.

It is also necessary to assure everyone that their standard of writing will not, in the end, deteriorate – that with practice they will improve their script and it will appear much more mature. The most problematic pupils are likely to be those who have been praised for their neat separate letters. An over emphasis on neatness is difficult to overcome.

In the next few pages the different families of joins are analysed separately.

Start joining in easy stages

If you have always printed, then you might like to start by feeling what it is like to write flowing, separate letters. This is the first group of letters with joining strokes at the base i l t u h m n a d.
They will help you to loosen up and change your movement. You can make patterns of these letters.

lllll unun nhnh mumu nhuy

Try words like 'mill', 'hunt', 'hum', 'hill' and 'nut' using only this group of letters. Write them faster and faster and you will soon find that you are joining up automatically. It is really easy this way.

un my tin hut it hut my hill minimum

Check the joining stroke at the base of your letters.

1 If it is too steep and jagged then your letters are too close together and get muddled up.

2 If it is too shallow then your writing becomes too spread out. Your joining stroke spaces your letters, so try to find a middle way. Then your writing will look even and be easy to read.

> r *hunt no*
> A steep up stroke - squashed letters.
>
> ι *hunt no*
> A medium up stroke - a happy medium.
>
> i *hunt no*
> A shallow up stroke - spread out letters.

You do not need to stop in the middle of short words to dot your 'i' and cross your 't'.

little little thin thin

You should write the whole word without stopping and then you can go back to finish off the bits.

Top joins are great time savers

If you want to demonstrate how joining letters saves time and energy top joins are a great way. Many people who consider that their handwriting is joined do not use top joins. Maybe they have not been taught how, and maybe it is not something that everyone would find out for themselves.

Show someone how to join two 'o's together then let them repeat it several times. It can be one of those magical moments when you make a real breakthrough.

A sentence like '*cook good food from our cookery book*' confirms the joined movement.

Left-handers need a special note here. Some of them find it quite impossible to go anti-clockwise around the letter 'o'. The only answer is to leave it unjoined – but it is always worth trying this 'oo' exercise in case it helps them to change.

As you can see from the examples, the top join from the letter 'r' is not always so simple owing to the many personal variations of the letter, nor is the join to the letter 'e'. Sometimes it is better to leave it unjoined. A little experimentation will soon sort that out.

Top joins are great time savers

The letters that join from the top are 'o' 'r' 'v' and 'w'.

Scribble a line of looped 'o's to get used to the feeling. Do it faster and faster. Forget about being neat. Now make patterns of the other letters that join from the top. Make sure you can tell 'r' from 'v'.

These words show how top joins vary with different styles of writing.

See what happens in the top of the 'r'.   Practise your letter 'r' before each vowel in turn.

You do not have to join an 'r' to the next letter.   These samples are better left unjoined.

Repairing bad joins.

These examples are self explanatory and would be useful to show to pupils who might have one or more of these faults. Some variations that would have been frowned on in the past are so practical that not only are they ignored but often recommended. An example is joining through the letter 'o' rather than going over the top and back.

Crossbar joins

An infant teacher once told me that the first join that she taught to her reception class was the crossbar join from the letter 'f'. Yet this join is seldom taught in junior school much to the detriment of writers. A simple crossbar join from 't' or 'f' allied to top joins lets the pen speed along smoothly. Try the words 'for' or 'top'.

Writers have to be careful to keep the crossbar along the midline and not to let it wander. After that there is plenty of scope for developing personal variations of crossbar joins to suit your own script. A light hearted way to encourage personal joins is to tell the writer not to lift the pen at all, even between words, during a whole sentence. This forces some unusual joins particularly crossbar ones. Try it yourself and make sure there are several 't's and 'f's in the sentence.

Repairing bad joins

Keep top joins straight. They must not wander up and down.

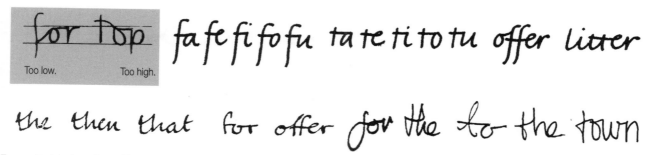

| art when
art when
Bad joins to tall letters. | hole hole
Do not slide over the top. | wound fónlcw
would follow
Wrong joins muddle words |
| Every two
Every two
Top joins must not droop. | live well
live well
Joins look like an extra letter. | wood waded
wood waded
Strokes lost in joining. |

Crossbar joins

Your crossbar must be at the right height. Not too high and not too low.

for top
Too low.   Too high.

fa fe fi fo fu   ta te ti to tu   offer litter

the   then   that   for   offer   for   the   to   the   town

Try crossbar joins to each vowel in turn. Then 'th', 'tt' and, 'ff' come next followed by short words.

Joins to the round group of letters

These examples illustrate how much easier it is to join to some letters if you have a narrow slanting script. With very fat letters it is tiresome and time consuming to go right over the top and back again. No wonder many people loop through the round letters instead. In some cases it is better to leave certain letters unjoined.

The letter 's' does not quite fit into the round family. Its only possible partner is 'f'. However it sometimes has joining problems as illustrated by the fat letters shown here. Two of these writers have made an attempt to simplify the letter, but it has not quite worked.

Some girls tend towards this extra wide form. Whether it is just peer group fashion or not it can be exaggerated to the point where it slows the writer and becomes a real nuisance. While not suggesting that you try to alter the proportions of every writer's letters, you could try this experiment. Pupils probably have at least two different ways of dealing with their names. The way they write their name at the top of any piece of work has often not changed for years and is usually relatively immature. Then there is the way they sign their name – when it is needed for official purposes. The written name may be even more childish than their usual script but often the writing contained in the signature is faster, more mature and has a more forward slant. The lesson is obvious. They already have the beginning of an adult script, but there is no guarantee that every teenager will heed it.

Joins to the round group of letters

These joins work best with oval slanting writing. With fat letters the join has to go over the top and back. Try the examples below to see what happens. A penlift may be better than an awkward join.

cacaca / *no vcicle*	*ad ag ad* / *dag gad add*	*adadad* / *how poor*
Fat letters, uneconomic joins.	Narrow letters, more efficient joins.	Round letters, looped joins.
hra bd had / *had world*	*chchch* / *church*	*eel uge* / *ed ige*
Good solution to a bad join.	Keep your 'c's round.	Some letters are better left unjoined.

ree nervant   glasses as   fish is

Do not pull 's' out of shape. Simplify it or do not join at all.

Looping at speed

When writers are relaxed loops from descenders can be an attractive part of their script. When they are tense this is the first stroke to become jagged and distorted. When it has been stressed too strongly that every letter must be joined to the next one you can find wonderful tangles as they try to deal with 'gg'. Another wasted movement occurs when the final descender is unnecessarily looped. There are no definite rules here. It is a matter for experimentation.

Fast personal joins

Personal joins are also all about experimenting. A good way to start is by explaining that different forms of a letter are not only permissible but desirable in different positions in the same word. This kind of exercise is successful in a whole class as well as one to one situation. Take the different forms of 'ff'. If several people produce their personal solution and then change paper with their neighbours they may find it impossible to replicate one another's efforts. That is when handwriting becomes interesting.

Half the battle is getting pupils to become engaged and interested in the subject, away from the usual battles over neatness and legibility. Their experiments with personal joins should lead to a maturer and, with luck, more efficient and faster script.

Looping at speed

Some letters will start to loop automatically when you write faster. It often pays to loop a descender at the beginning of a word, and sometimes in the middle. It is a waste, however, to put a loop on a final letter.

jog   jog   jogging   ing

You loop some of your descenders when you write fast, but not the final one.

Fast personal joins

Now your writing is ready to speed up. Your joins are becoming automatic, but you may not always use the same ones. These sets of words on the right will show you why.

You can find one form of a letter at the beginning of a word and another in the middle or at the end. You plan several letters in advance when you are writing fast. The shape of a letter, therefore depends on what was written before and what comes next. Your hand may need a penlift after writing several complex movements. You start again with a simpler letter, so even double letters are not always identical.

This is the kind of variation that makes handwriting interesting.

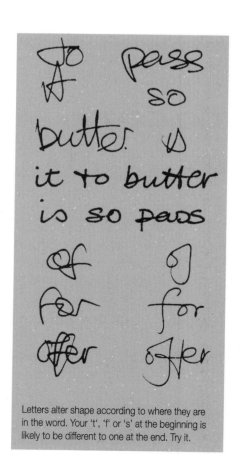

Letters alter shape according to where they are in the word. Your 't', 'f' or 's' at the beginning is likely to be different to one at the end. Try it.

Letters and joins for left-handers

Some left-handers show great ingenuity in devising forms that compensate for their natural directionality. This makes it easier for them to proceed from right to left in particular when they make a horizontal stroke. Look at the example below that shows an ingenious way of starting the letter 't' in the initial position. It was devised by a primary school child. The 'ff' in giraffe and the crossbars in the example below it are also interesting. No one had taught them these solutions, but they work. The letters 'f' and 's' can cause problems too as they include a counterchange movement (a change of direction in the middle of a letter). All these examples would give pupils ideas on how to make life simpler for themselves.

Some joins are difficult for left-handers and it seems reasonable to suggest that individuals might leave those that distort their writing. That brings us on to something that is not illustrated here. As well as problems with the right to left movement anti-clockwise movements can be difficult. It may be almost impossible for some left-handers to write the letter 'o' the correct way round. The kindest thing may be to understand that they are not being wilful. As long as they do not try to join from that letter it will neither be noticeable nor disadvantage the writer.

One left-handed boy who had severe directional problems was told to slow down in order to make his writing more legible. The trouble was that the momentum involved in writing fast helped his strokes to go in the accepted direction. When he slowed down admittedly his writing was neater but every possible stroke went right to left and clockwise. We can only learn from such pupils.

Letters and joins for left-handers

Some of the movements involved in writing our alphabet are awkward for left-handers. Try this simple test; draw two straight lines in opposite directions. Most left-handers find the top one far easier. That is why almost all left-handers cross their 'f' and 't' from right to left. Crossbar joins may well feel strange.

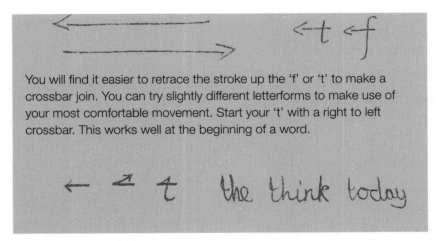

You will find it easier to retrace the stroke up the 'f' or 't' to make a crossbar join. You can try slightly different letterforms to make use of your most comfortable movement. Start your 't' with a right to left crossbar. This works well at the beginning of a word.

The letters 'f' and 's' can be awkward because they change direction in the middle. Try simplifying them. Experiment until you find something that suits you.

If you have to push uphill to join to round letters you might find it easier not to bother. Lift your pen more often and your handwriting might be easier to read. Changing your hand position can also make things better. See page 27.

Retrace your stroke then it will be easier to join from the crossbar.

left-handerss find ingenious ways to deal with crossbars. Try these two.

Simplify the letters f and s. This writer made both letters more efficient.

Awkward joins to round letters.

How far can you go with letters?

The first set of examples below includes the use of personalised letters such as a Greek 'e' or a typographic 'a'. They are getting out of hand at speed. The second set are likely to be the exaggerated result of two different models. The third set is typical of young teenage girls and in the fourth the flourished descenders need to disappear as do the over-large loops in the final one.

None of these issues are easy to deal with. Individuals who have developed flamboyant or eccentric letters are probably only reflecting their own characteristics. It may not be the best approach to criticise them but something has to be done. Praise for originality might work but only in the context of suitable usage. As well as being a reflection of the writer's individuality, these forms were perhaps copied from someone they admire or possibly a peer group style. This may be perfectly acceptable in letters to their friends. For formal work they need simplifying for the sake of legibility if nothing else.

A head teacher in a local secondary school once said that she was going to ban circles on the top of 'o's. My reply was that she might as well ban measles. Those circles, as with the other styles below, were a sign of immaturity and, with luck, would disappear as the girls grew up. Let your pupils laugh at the examples and suggest their solutions.

How far can you go with letters?

Keep the basic shape of your letters conventional.
You do not want to have the same writing as everyone else but if you want people to be able to read it easily then you have got to keep within certain limits. As well as the list on page 40 there are other things to watch.

Adults do not read every letter of every word. They scan the general shape of the word, but when they come to a mixture of unusual shapes they have to stop and puzzle it out. Simple letters can be personalised and still be recognisable at speed, but unusual letter shapes cause confusion.

'a' and 'e' get the worst treatment.

You need to keep the essence of each letter, so do not lose the differences between 'n' and 'u'.

'u' and 'n' arches must look different.

The letter 'i' should have a dot and not a large circle. These circles can get so exaggerated that they suggest another letter.

Circles on top of 'i' look silly.

Those squiggles that are used to decorate 'g' and 'y' are also best kept for personal correspondence. They may be fun, but distract the reader and make your hand move in the wrong direction. An economical movement looks better and works better too.

Squiggles are confusing.

Loops can get out of hand and your handwriting can end up looking like knitting.

Muddled loops. This says 'should at all'.

Fast writing and slow writing

It is important for all pupils to understand the need for different speeds and standards of writing for different tasks. Many people do not realise the effect of writing at different speeds on their script so this exercise can be useful in many ways.

The most efficient writers have already worked this out for themselves, indeed if their script is very efficient, perhaps narrow and slanting, there may be little visible difference when they reach their maximum speed. They are lucky. In the case of special needs teachers your pupils may need more guidance. By asking anyone to perform the simple exercises shown below both they and you will learn. Your pupils' perception of what comprises best handwriting might differ from yours. Sometimes their fastest writing is the most mature, sometimes it is a disaster. Either way it is a good starting point for discussion.

You may also need to discuss when the different levels are most appropriate. Print script need not be derided. It is useful for labelling maps and diagrams, but it becomes tiring on the wrist when written at speed. It can also appear immature. Fast writing is still still necessary in order to get enough down in an examination and very fast scribble usually is adequate for notes that only the writer needs to read.

Fast writing and slow writing

This is my very best hand writing.

the   the the the the the

This is my fastest scribble

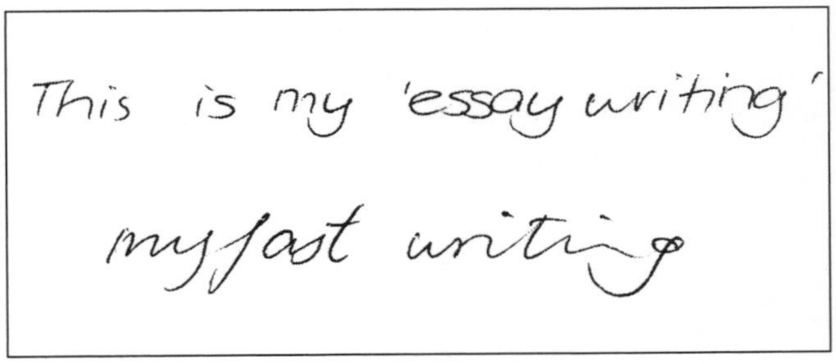

This is my 'essay writing'

my fast writing

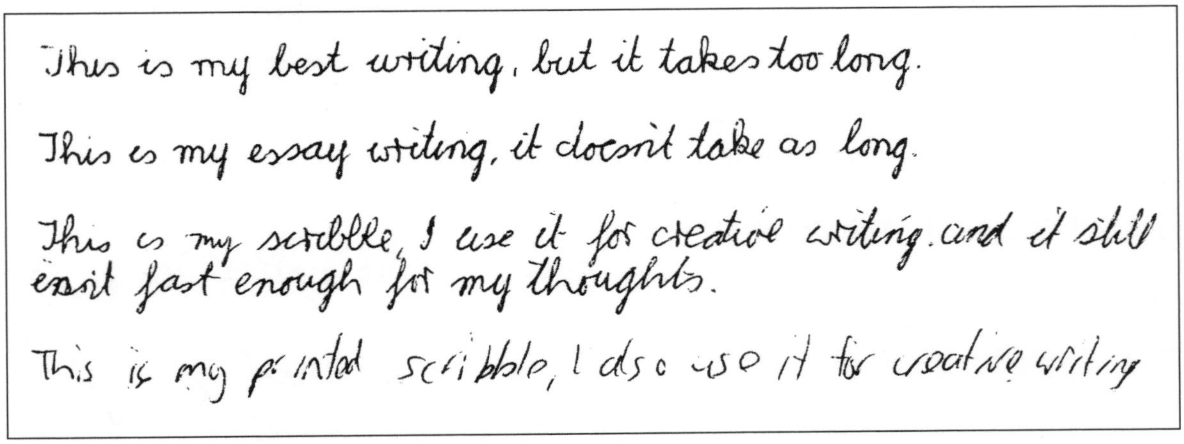

This is my best writing, but it takes too long.

This is my essay writing, it doesn't take as long.

This is my scribble, I use it for creative writing and it still
isn't fast enough for my thoughts.

This is my printed scribble, I also use it for creative writing

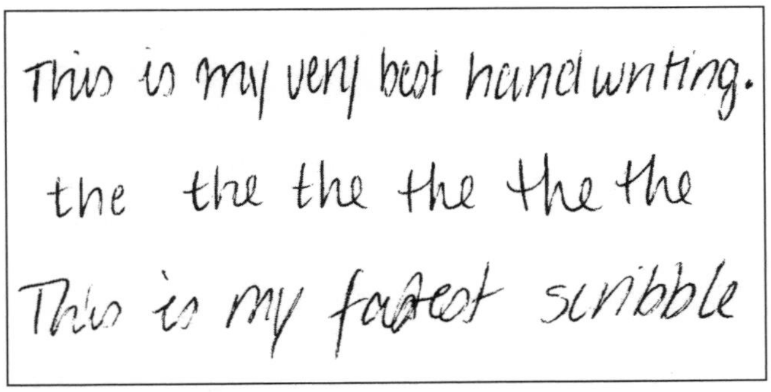

Your slant, his slant, no slant

The way letters slant is governed by the way the pen is held and this is tied up with the way writers use their body. If someone wants substantially to alter their slant they will have to alter the rotation of their wrist. That sounds complicated but conversely as the slant of letters is consciously altered the wrist would alter automatically. Try it out yourself. This is illustrated and explained more fully on page 27. On page 30 you can see how the alternative pen hold can alter the slant of letters. Changing a left-hander from an inverted hand position will do the same. See page 35.

Having said all that there is in fact no particular reason to suggest that anyone should alter the slant of their writing unless it is so extreme that it makes the script hard to read.

When handwriting slants at many different angles that usually indicates a different problem. It is most likely the effect of tension. It is hard to explain but the hand gets jerky and the result is that the regular slant of the writing is disrupted. Difficulty with spelling or grammar can be enough to make the writer hesitate and worry between words. That might be the cause. On the next page it is explained how tension can disrupt spacing. All these factors are linked together, and like everything involved with tension you can help the writer relax. Try using the relaxing exercises on page 33, and see the effect. Sometimes these exercises reveal a pupil's natural slant. See page 72. It is much more difficult to ensure whatever you do in a one to one situation will last when the writer is in a tense environment.

Your slant, his slant, no slant

The most practical letters slope slightly forward. Join easily and speed up well. But like everything else, slant is a personal matter.
You need a consistent but not too pronounced angle for efficient, legible handwriting. Upright letters may work well for you, but even then you may find that they tilt forward a little when you go really fast.

Many left-handers and some right-handers have a writing that slopes slightly backwards. This seems to annoy some people but as long as the backward slant is slight and consistent it should not slow down too much or affect legibility. Too much slant, either backwards or forwards, does make writing harder to read. Try to avoid this.

Handwriting that slants in different directions is not only distracting to read but suggests that the writer may be confused too. If your writing is a mixture of backward, upright and forward strokes then try to make your up your mind which slant suits you best. Practise until one angle becomes natural. You can rule yourself some slant-lines for a while to encourage regularity.

Look at page 27. It explains how your hand position can affect the slant of your writing. Change your hand position and you change your slant.

and honey
my smile

Whatever your angle, be consistent.

mainly
in the is
ideas seen,
more time

Too much slant either way is hard to read.

The only way to
/ lie awake and
afraid to go to
ery night is hell.

A mixture of slants is distracting.

How much space is enough?

There are no definite rules about spacing. It is really a matter of common sense and depends largely on the size of writing. You need enough space to separate words – fat, spread out writing needs more space than small, compact writing. This is easy in typography where letterforms are regular and easier to read. There the space is usually the same size as a letter, for instance an 'm' for a wide space or an 'n' space when you want closer packed text. It is like the space bar on a keyboard.

The two bottom examples below might cause alarm. Why does the girl with the small writing leave such large spaces? There would be rivers of white all down the page making a disturbing pattern. One such writer, when questioned, answered that it was easier to read. She had been criticised because her small writing was difficult to read and this was her solution. On the other hand maybe this girl had been taught to space by using her thumb to measure the gaps between words. It is always worth asking 'why' before suggesting possible remedies.

At the very bottom of the page is the kind of script that disturbs me most. Some words are well written, even mature like 'his', while others are almost illegible. The hand barely moves sometimes and then jerks and repositions after a huge gap. What deep tension could be causing this? This writer does not need criticism but sympathetic questioning. All these insights into what handwriting is indicating are not making your job any easier. They may, however, help you to understand and assist some of your most troubled pupils.

How much space is enough?

It is difficult to give rules about spacing joined up letters. They must hold together as words but each letter must be separately recognisable. You need to space your words out enough to be able to tell where one ends and the next begins. That is obvious – but how much space is enough? It is common sense.

Large, loosely spaced letters need more space between words than smaller and more compact ones. The space between words varies with the size of the letter and width of joining stroke. That is why it does not work too well when people with tiny writing try to make it more legible by leaving large gaps between words. It only breaks the page up and makes matters worse.

neatoprintoscript   with o joined o writing
neat print script   with joined writing

The space of an 'o' of the same size as the writing is sufficient for print script. For cursive writing, it is safer to say that you need the space of an 'o' with enough room for a joining stroke on each side. It is all related to your writing, but when the spaces are too wide white patches all down the page will distract the reader.

Some of you may remember being taught to use a thumb or finger to space between letters. At five years old you may have been told to place it on the paper. later on you used it as a mental spacer. Forget that lesson. Your thumb has grown with age and your writing has shrunk. Your spaces would be huge.

Most of the i
the only town

Fat writing, wide spacing.

living mainly by fishing.
the only town on the is

Smaller writing, closer spacing.

small   island   whose   inhabi
town   on   the   island   als

Small writing, rather wide spaces.

ore   and   yo
Blot   when   his
Le   ren   all

Much too wide word spacing.

Spiky letters or round letters

Your handwriting is a mixture of what you were taught and who you are. Who you are is a mix of your character and the way your body works. No style of writing can be judged as being better than any other. In the nineteenth century, for instance, everyone was taught a strict model, and most people's writing remained similar throughout their lives. Even so, forceful characters like Nelson or imaginative people like Constable broke free and developed their own personal script.

The two people whose writing is illustrated below are both artists. One of them is left-handed. Some people will like one and dislike the other, but they are both examples of good handwriting. Sometimes it is hard to appreciate a script that is very different from your own. Sometimes you know that a certain style is unlikely to develop into a mature and efficient way – but it is seldom a good idea to intervene.

In the secondary school, pupils are changing and experimenting all the time. Some of these experimental forms were shown on page 48. Some schools believe that exposing pupils to good examples of calligraphy will influence them. Please do not let me discourage you, but teenagers are just as likely to gravitate towards the style of an admired friend or teacher.

Spiky letters or round letters

Why are there so many differently shaped letters and different kinds of handwriting? It is partly because of what we have been taught. There are so many models and each one is what someone at some time decided the ideal letter shape should be. Teachers know that good, clear writing will help a student to get on. They cannot be blamed for trying to get you to write well in the conventional sense. However, many people will not follow a conventional model. A very tense person may also be unable to do so. When it comes to style, what one person admires the next person may hate. That is why this book stresses the need for an efficient personal handwriting and does not suggest any special model.

A pointed personal italic.

A more rounded cursive.

Our handwriting is also part of what we are like ourselves and how our arm and body works. Quite understandably we like our own kind of writing, though sometimes we might like to be a bit better at it. That is where the problem lies. A son who wants to be an artist or perhaps a footballer, is unlikely to have the same writing as a father who works in a bank. He probably has quite different tastes and interests. A girl who might want to be a hairdresser or perhaps a bio-chemist, will probably be a different kind of person with different writing from her English teacher. One is not right and the other wrong. They are just different.

Mixed-up models

However hard they try some children find their school model impossible to follow. Italic handwriting can be efficient, legible and to many people beautiful, and many of those taught italic retain it for life. On the other hand it can be disastrous for some children. The word children is used here rather than pupils because few secondary schools enforce a strict model today.

Italic does not come naturally to everyone, teachers included. Some people perceive and produce its subtle exit stroke as too acute. That zig zag movement can result in an illegible tangle when performed at speed. The pupil who wrote the example below had to be shown that a more naturally curved exit was not only better for his writing but his natural movement. The usual pattern of *ilililil* did the trick.

There may be another unintended consequence of italic. Students can be well taught and come to view italic as a beautiful and desirable style. Some pupils, however, may not have the skill to adapt it to a fast hand. These individuals then suffer later on by neither being able to write fast enough for examination purposes, nor change their perception of what is a desirable script. They may need to become more flexible in their attitude to standards of handwriting for everyday purposes.

Mixed-up models

There are so many styles taught in our schools that it is no wonder that some of you end up in a muddle.

At one extreme there is italic. The word italic is meant to describe oval, slightly slanted letters. These letters are often taught with a broad-edged nib. This is supposed to make it easier, but with some young children their italic ends up being too jagged. Then it is difficult to read.

This is 'minimum' upside down.

Zig zag writing is difficult to read.

You can exercise your way out of a jagged movement.

Before

Loosen up your letter group by group.

After

Any style can become exaggerated. Look at your writing with this in mind. Have you ended up with a strange assortment of letters? This can happen to anyone who has had to change schools and models several times. The actual shape of your letters and the different angle of joining strokes can cause uneven writing. Divide your letters into family groups and see if this helps you to sort out a more unified alphabet for yourself.

Some round letters are too round

At the other extreme from italic there are many early models with rounded letterforms. While once again suggesting that it is unwise to criticise a particular style there is no harm in pointing out the problems that sometimes develop. Undoubtedly very round letters are less efficient when joined or written at speed. Then again there is a problem with those pupils, like the first example below, who were so proud of their ability to follow the primary school model that they find it difficult to move forward. They would seldom be criticised for the legible appearance of their writing at any stage, but their script remains rather immature. They are also reluctant to speed up for fear of spoiling their much admired handwriting.

As you can see in the lower examples some rounded letterforms are prone to distort at speed. The open 'b' and 'p' are the worst, but the 'a', 'c' and 'g' family of letters also get dragged open in an attempt to write fast. It is worth drawing a writer's attention to these drawbacks of the model.

You will also come across pupils from abroad who may have learned quite different styles. They will have enough trouble adjusting to a new educational system without having to alter their handwriting. Some teachers may have difficulty reading their homework but it would be unkind to make too much of it. They may well copy their classmates in time without any outside prompting – if they think it a good idea.

✂ ───

Some round letters are too round

At the other extreme there are rounded, simplified cursive models. They are meant to teach five- and six-year-olds to join up easily. They do this job very well, sometimes too well. Some of these children are left for life with the idea that they must join all their letters all the time, even though their style of letters make it difficult. See also page 45.

island made up of by volcanic erupti

This is like the model. Every letter joins. It is clear but slow, and rather childish.

made land who small

See the awkward joins to 'a', 'o' and 'd'. A pen lift would be quicker than joining.

island whose lies a small rock

Some people go back to separate letters when their joins do not work well.

ring morning

Rounded letters can open out at speed. Narrower writing often works best.

The simplified rounded letters deteriorate at speed. The open 'b', 'p' and 'r' are worst.

real places more paintings really.

Careless writing mixes 'n', 'r' and 'p'.

by by ly

'b' loses its shape and sometimes looks like 'l'.

opposed people

This open 'p' does not do well at speed.

by bptop r

Close 'b' and 'p' and dip the top of 'r'.

Large writing and small writing

There are as many misconceptions and misunderstandings about size as any other factor involved in handwriting. First of all, individual pupils may have a completely different concept of size to you. They may not see their writing as particularly large or small at all. Some people associate small with neat, while others think it might be quicker to write small. Neither are particularly true; it is more time consuming to write very small and still retain legibility. The writer of the first small example is a calligrapher and has sufficient hand control to write both fast and legibly, but the second one has sacrificed any attempt at joining in order to appear neat. It requires both great agility and efficient letterforms for small scripts to succeed.

Over-large letters present other problems and have different causes. The unfortunate boy who produced the final example had enlarged his writing because his teacher had said that his writing was illegible. He thought making it larger would help. What he needed was some help with the movement of some of his letters. If nothing else, wider line spacing would have helped both the over-large writers.

Some of the causes of either over-large or tiny writing can be put down to certain characteristics of the writers, but not all. Questions, as usual, are a vital part of understanding, before offering advice.

Large writing and small writing

The size of your writing is a personal matter but there are limits. Small writing must be clear and well spaced or it will be hard to read. Tiny writing can be a sign of tension. Relax and it gets larger. Over-large writing gets muddled as the lines mesh together.

it was most pleasant to stay for dinner. I did enjoy meeting and talking with your family— not that I was able to as much as I'd have liked

island made up of rock formed

Small letters must be clear and well spaced.

Complex or careless writing is illegible when small.

Try to control the size of your letters so there is space between the lines of writing.

Many of these letters are wrongly formed. Making them larger does not make them any more legible.

Spot your own mistakes

This part of the book is the most suitable for giving out to those pupils who you think will be able to sort out their own problems once they can see where they are going wrong. It is also useful for those pupils who are shy or too defensive to benefit from more direct help at first. As many of these problems have been analysed on previous pages here are some suggestions for useful exercises or sentences for the errors that appear on this page. With wrongly formed letters start with separate letters before progressing to joined up. With the joined typeface used here you would easily be able to type out a relevant letter pattern or sentence. You and your pupils may think of better sentences.

cdcdcdcd adadadad The mad dad cannot add Bad ladders had added to danger

cdcdcdcd adadadad The mad Dad cannot add. Bad ladders had added to danger.

ococococo oooooo Row row row our boat Cook books to cook good food

ocococot oooooooo Row row row our boat. Cook books to cook good food.

cscscscs cfscfscfscfs Please pass us some sausages She is so sorry she missed us

cscscscs cfscfscfscfs Please pass us some sausages. She is so sorry she missed us.

hphphphp hbphbphbp Top up the penny pot. Tip up Pip's poppy plant's pot

hphphphp hbhbhbhb Top up the penny pot. Tip up Pip's poppy plant's pot.

Spot your own mistakes

Use this part of the book for fault finding. Skim through the pages and look for samples that show what is wrong with your writing. This will help you to understand your faults. Putting them right will then be much easier.

formed

Wrongly formed letters join badly.

lots to worry
no more to cp

They get more confused when written fast.

Wrongly constructed letters

The 'o' goes round the wrong way. Left-handers often do this.

Correct the movement this way.

This 's' starts at the wrong place. The 'p' starts correctly but then goes mad. It was easy to alter the 's' to start at the top but 'p' took longer.

The 'b' helped 'p' to move properly.

Unevenly sized letters

The writing of the girl who produced the top line of examples is typical of pupils with coordination difficulties. Their hands do not work well enough to manage the complex movement of some letters in the same space as the simple ones. Letters such as 's' and 'k' indicate that they are the ones that need simplifying by protruding above the line and giving the script an uneven appearance. Experiment with the different forms: kkk to find which one is easiest then perhaps try this exercise: kkk kkk ckck ckckck then 'Jack kicked the bucket back'. You can see that she slightly simplified her 's' straight away after an explanation. Exercises such as those suggested on the facing page, would help anyone to find the form that suits their script and to realise that there can be different forms in different positions. A full 's' works well in the initial position half 's's work better in the middle. This particular girl made some improvements but she still has some way to go. She needs to close her 'p' and sort out her descenders.

The next two pupils also need help to find satisfactory solutions to 'k' and 's'. They are fast writers and are cutting too many corners.

On the bottom row you will see three different manifestations of uneven letters. The first boy has a script that typifies tension. The jagged strokes and different sizes reflect his problems. The middle writing is distorted by bad joins and possibly joining too much, and the last shows how bad print, involving constant repositioning, can result in uneven heights.

Unevenly sized letters

Letters that are different sizes make your writing uneven. They get out of line and distract the reader. The most usual culprits are 's' and 'k'. They are complex letters that have several changes of direction to make in a small space.

Spent donsha / *known like tree*	*times lots as* / *tick like looked*	*those same* / *paint nart*
The letters 's' and 'k' are too tall. A less complicated movement will help.	Simplify them or practise until they work better for you.	Sometimes bad joins make letters like this 's' stick out, so lift your pen instead. The 'p' needs attention too.
there slower strokes		*better brown*
This writer must slow down. He is going so fast that he cannot control the 's' in the word 'these' or complete the 'k' in 'strokes'.		Don't cut too many corners at speed. 'better known' reads as 'better brown'.
me slowly / *t her hand over* / *self screaming*	*to consde him* / *cows vanished*	*and time* / *thing*
Tension can distort your writing and make your letters vary in size. Relax.	Bad joins can push your letters out of line. Those 'c's, 'o's and 's' are the worst.	You can get careless about the heights of letters if you do not join.

Where does one letter end and the next begin?

This page is the one that should have the most immediate effect on those whose faults are illustrated here. It should help by making them laugh at the various mistakes. Most of these muddles are caused by pupils who do not join their letters but who think that if they squash them close enough together no one will notice. Most of them still have straight print script letters with no exit strokes. They first need to learn separate letters with exit strokes.

They then could copy the words: *coin gang ant loud clock close side* and compare with the examples as the exit strokes will automatically space their letters. Then they can try to join up. For 'k's that are falling apart, after seeing if one of the three 'k's on the previous page might suit them better, then they could try the sentence '*Jack is kicking the bucket back*'.

Although there are no examples here of actual mirror image there are several that illustrate how similar the shapes of our letters are, so 'cl' easily becomes 'd' and 'lo' can look like 'b'. Should you have a pupil who still confuses 'b' and 'd' these repetitive exercise and sentences that might help them.

bdbdbdbd bad bed bad bed bad bed A bumpy bed is bad but a hard bed is a bad bed too.

Some pupils have never had the opportunity to compare the 'mirror image' letters. It is not only 'b' and 'd'.

b	d		u	n
p	q		h	y

✄

Where does one letter end and the next begin?

Leave enough space between separate letters so you can tell where one ends and the next begins. Good joining strokes will then regulate the spacing for you. Sometimes complex letters like 'k' fall apart, making matters worse.

Are these words 'coin' or 'can', 'going' or 'gang'?

Are these words 'ant' or 'art'. 'loud' 'lad' or 'bud'? This happens when letters are too close.

'clock' or 'dock'?

'close' or 'dose'?

'backs' or 'bad is', 'king' or 'icing'? A loose 'k' and tight 'cl' do this.

'side' or 'sick'?

'down' or 'clown'?

Enlarging handwriting does not solve bad letter spacing.

A bad start. This writing is squashed together to look as if it joins.

Squashed writing gets more confusing as it becomes complex and personal.

Careless letters make bad spacing more serious. The letters 'ds' could be 'cb' or 'clo'.

Rounded letters overlap and get muddled.

Unconventional forms make matters worse.

Zig zag strokes make a confusing pattern.

Are your ascenders too long or too short?

Looking at these two different styles with over-long ascenders you have to wonder how they have come about, A graphologist might have some interesting views! You might have some difficulty curbing the exuberance of someone who writes like the person who produced the top example. The lower writer, with the curly ascenders, reacted well to suggestions that simplification was a good idea. Sometimes practising just one word is enough to sort things out; others may need a sentence or even several sentences.

Try: 'The half full black bottle' or 'I did little but fly back'.

It is probably more difficult to make alterations to the lower two examples. Both writers have the usual signs of immaturity in their script and both are making restricted movements with their hand. The first reacted well to the sequence 'itl itl' but you might find that it takes some time before a pupil who writes like this is able to free up her writing to make a marked alteration when engaged in her everyday work.

The same would apply to the last example which has such a definite and truncated movement. First you would need to persuade the writer of the advantages of joining up. For someone with straight letters that terminate with considerable pressure on the baseline it is not easy to relax that pressure and at the same time change direction to add an exit stroke to a letter. This needs to be sorted out before dealing with the differing heights of her letters with appropriate sequences then words.

This pupil is a perfect example of the dangers of teaching children print letters, rather than those with exit strokes. No doubt this writer's script always appeared neat and she may never even have tried to join up.

Are your ascenders too long or too short?

Your ascenders must be long enough for there to be a distinct difference between tall and short letters but not so long that lines of writing get tangled up with each other.

Long ascenders collide with the line above.

Shorter ascenders – more legible writing.

Looped ascenders disrupt the flow of the writing.

A simpler movement – clearer more efficient writing.

Ascenders must not get too short.

Allow for the three heights of letters. The letter 'l' should be taller than 't'.

Short ascenders confuse letters such as 'h' and 'n', or even 'a' and 'd'.

These sequences show the difference that adequate ascenders can make.

Are your descenders causing confusion?

By now you will be familiar with the techniques of letter patterns and appropriate words to help correct the common faults. Perhaps it is time to think a bit more about what these different examples are suggesting about the writer. The first line of examples illustrates how abrupt descenders are confusing but do not suggest a serious problem. They might be the result of a misinterpreted italic or other model which leaves a writer with jagged joining strokes. It was easy to show this boy how a more relaxed join resulted in a happier script. He was delighted.

The next three are quite different. These exuberant and exaggerated descenders may be the pride and joy of the writer. It may not be easy to persuade them to change. Depending on what, if any, other problems they might have in school, it might be better to ignore the descenders and hope the writers grow out of them.

The bottom three examples are more worrying. Each of these writers has unhappy writing. They all loop the ascender at the end of a word which, allied to their ugly descenders, makes their writing even worse. Tenseness is distorting all their script, but in different ways. You will be able to do little until you can get them to relax. Then you could sort out the descenders – or with luck they might improve by themselves as body and hand relax. You will be left only to praise the result and then suggest leaving the last letter unlooped. In circumstances like these praise can have a miraculous effect.

✂

Are your descenders causing confusion?

joyful ally you jot	*g got ing*	*you got got jot jot jot jot*
These descenders join but don't loop.	This 'g' looks more like a 'q'.	Loops sort out the confusion.
2 needing you nay sleeping... re ffends know	*living mainly by fishing*	*ainly by the inhab*
Descenders can get out of hand.	These flourishes just look fussy.	Larger flourishes get in a tangle.
Suddenly walking again	*very tight only got*	*living mainly by fishing.*
These are tense, cramped descenders. Try to relax.	These descenders are too short to loop happily.	These final letters would be better unlooped.

Dealing with descenders

This page is getting down to the details of the pleasurable activity of redesigning a couple of letters in an otherwise more or less satisfactory script. Most pupils react very positively to this. It is unlikely that the boy whose work is represented on this page was in a special needs group. If you were to have a handwriting club – purely voluntary – this is the kind of activity that takes little time, works wonders and also stimulates others to experiment.

You can see how it worked. First we attended to his 'y' which was at a different angle to the rest of his letters. His separate letter was fine but it did not work so well when joined. Then it became apparent that his 'f' needed help. You can see that he got a bit worried and his writing deteriorated as he tensed up. We went back to separate letters, simplified the 'f' and suddenly it all worked. There were relaxed descenders, a very efficient 'f' and even the 's' seemed to sort itself out. He was delighted and it was only to be hoped that the improvement was lasting. With luck his teachers would notice and praise him for the improvement.

Dealing with descenders

1 These descenders are at a different angle to the rest of the writing.

First develop good separate letters to suit the rest of your writing.

Practise them in groups of letters such as common word endings.

Try words with several descenders.

Repeat until they work well.

The 'f' crossbar is still too low.

2 New 'f's and 's's are needed here. These words are meant to be 'suffer' and 'fist'.

How to design a simpler, well shaped 'g' with the help of its letter family.

Simplify the 'f'. It should be at the same angle as the other letters.

Descenders suffer as the writing gets small and tense.

The new 'g' now works well when looped.

What a difference after just a few minutes' practice.

Are you leaving strokes out?

This page provides another close look at common faults. A scooped 'u' is a legacy from uncorrected print in the early years. It seems odd that this writer cannot see how both his 'u' and 's' are holding him back. It should be easy to show this particular writer how much more easily his writing will flow for him, and how much better his script will look. That is because some of his other letters are particularly well formed so you can start by praising them. Exercises could be *uy uy* then *up up* and when he has mastered a half 's' perhaps *us us us*. You or he might enjoy working out a better sentence than *'Put up your bus pass'*!

Another fault from the same cause is leaving out all the strokes in the rnm group. The pupil may laugh at the wound/around confusion but it may not be so easy to alter all these letters in a not very mature script. The next pupil has the same faults magnified by the attempts to join every letter. They both will need to practise the sequences shown below until the movement feels more natural and they are convinced of its benefit. Then they can try a sentence like *'slamming my door jammed it'* or *'winning a running race is fun'*. Both of them need to practise in separate letters before attempting to join.

The middle two appear more immature. That certainly does not apply to the bottom example – not that this will make it any easier to deal with. He or she has the same fault but partially covers it up with a mature very fast handwriting and may even think that truncated letters help to speed it up. You will have quite a job persuading this writer of the benefits of alterations. Your best hope would be to avoid the criticism – even though the script is nearly impossible to decipher. Remember, handwriting problems are not necessarily a problem of low achievers, in fact they can have serious consequences for the high flying student.

Are you leaving strokes out?

Letters that have a stroke missing are misleading. You must deal with them. This shows you how.

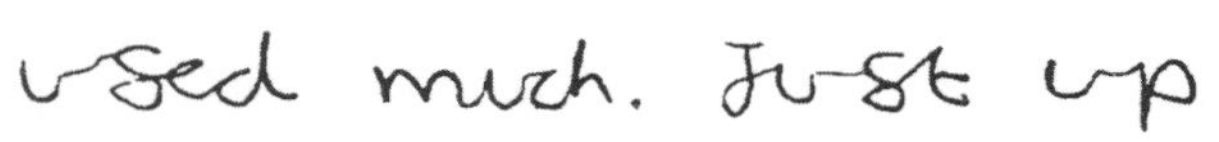

This 'u' cannot join properly because the final downstroke is missing.

The vital downstroke is missing from 'r'. The word 'around' looks like 'wound'.

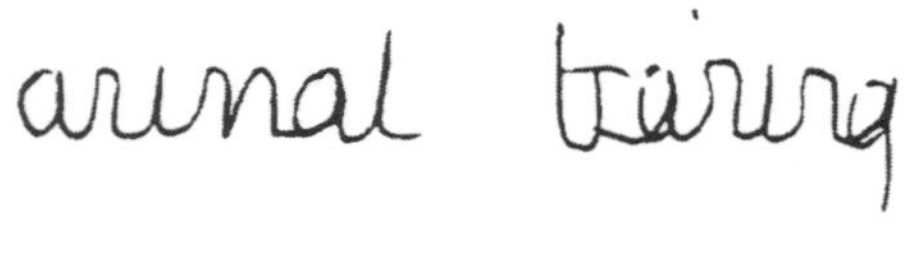

The first stroke is left off 'n', 'm' and 'r' in 'animal training'. The 'm' then looks like 'n'.

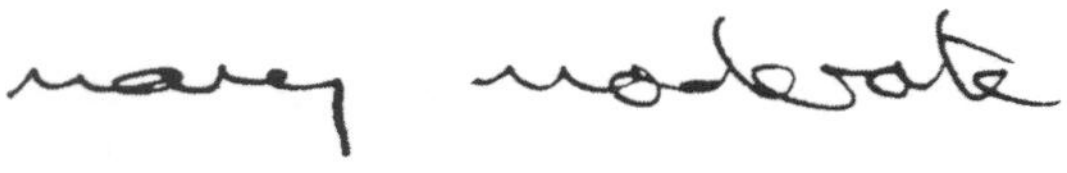

No downstrokes on 'm' and 'n'. More confusing still with small personal handwriting.

More missing strokes

The examples on this page look more closely at some more of the problems that were listed in the twelve points of legibility on page 40. They show the effects of uncompleted and distorted joining strokes. Letters must be distinctly separated. Melting somehow into the next letter causes wonderful confusion.

The first example shows some adequate joins and then spoils it. Here you could try *ayayay* then the words *way* and *day*. Look at any text that she has written and you will probably find a few other instances of similar errors. Then between you, make up short sentences to include words using those other joins.

The second pupil needs similar treatment. She may be having trouble with other top joining letters as well as 'w'. Try *vnvnvn* as well as *wnwnw* before a sentence like: *'Our own rowers row very well'*.

The next script will need a bit of sorting out. I am sure the girl thinks it very decorative but with an incomplete 'u' which curls over the top of very short descenders it becomes hard to decipher. Her Greek 'd' is quite acceptable at the end of a word. First sort out her 'u' with the usual uyuyuy then help her to straighten her l with *ililil*, and her heights with *iltiltiltilt*. 'Little' is a good word for her. It might be more successful for this girl to copy one of her own sentences so she can compare the difference between her reformed writing and her original.

The next pupil does not complete the 'h'. This can be dealt with by the sequences *hnhnhnhn* and *henhenhenhen*. After that she can copy her own sentence starting: *'When she brushed her hair'*.

The final pupil has got to learn to complete the letter 'a' before proceeding. Try *alalal* before *atatat* and *'the cat sat on the mat'*.

More missing strokes

away days

A stroke is missing between 'a' and 'y'.

was flour

A 'w' without a space or a joining stroke looks like 'u'.

out ward

Incomplete 'u' joins badly making 'out' and 'would' illegible.

when she brushed

Unfinished 'h' slides carelessly into the next letter.

cat sat on mat

Sloppy 'a' without proper downstroke looks like 'o'.

day day
uy uy ay ay way day

our own
wowo wnwn wawa

and ould
uy uy ulul utut ulul

ked hed
hnhnhn hnhe hehehehe

cat at
alalal aiaiai aoaoao

Exit but not entry strokes

So far this book has not commented on the many different handwriting models in use in our primary schools. The only factor mentioned has been the advantage of separate letters with exit strokes over the straight, abrupt letters of print script. However, recently there has been a fashion for reverting to using entry strokes such as is still taught in America. You can see below what happens if anyone who has been taught to use entry strokes takes a pen lift in the middle of a long word, something that is necessary with modern writing implements. Here letters that join from the top like 'o', 'r', 'v' and 'w' are not meeting up with letters that start on the baseline. The last letter of the letter sequences looks like a bad join from an 'a' but is actually 'ori'.

Apart from being more complex to learn it must be more time consuming to write the extra stroke. The only argument in its favour is that it is good for those with complex learning difficulties to start every letter on the baseline. For that reason alone all other pupils are disadvantaged. It certainly is not an aid to joining up, and it is easy for nearly everyone to understand that all letters start at the top except 'e' and 'd'.

The samples below are from relatively mature writers. The first one is faking the entry strokes and must have come from a very strict school where there was criticism for anyone who did not follow the school model – or he or she just thinks it clever. The last writer was delighted to be rid of his entry strokes, and you can sense it in his script.

Exit but not entry strokes

This page shows why letters with entry strokes are inefficient and only lead to trouble. It is a pity that they are still taught. Some letters finish at the base line; these will join to entry strokes. Other letters finish at the top; this is where it all goes wrong.

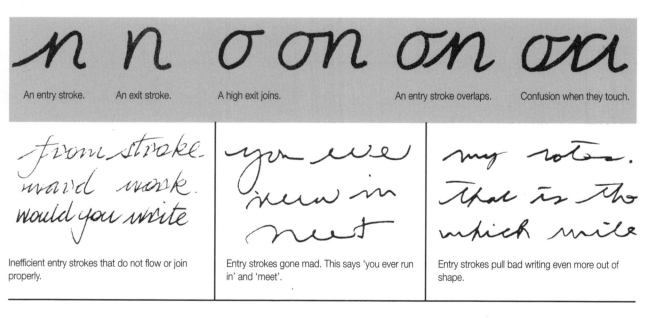

| An entry stroke. | An exit stroke. | A high exit joins. | An entry stroke overlaps. | Confusion when they touch. |

Inefficient entry strokes that do not flow or join properly.

Entry strokes gone mad. This says 'you ever run in' and 'meet'.

Entry strokes pull bad writing even more out of shape.

It is never easy to change a writing habit. This pupil discards entry strokes then can enjoy efficient top joins.

Exit strokes: a recipe for disaster

Once a child has been taught that an entry stroke is an integral part of a letter, like any other aspect of handwriting, it becomes an automated habit and is difficult to alter. You can see that entry strokes caused similar problems a hundred years ago when the pointed quills or nibs and the copperplate writing made entry strokes necessary. Then, the entry stroke helped to get the ink to flow. It was not a good idea to stop in the middle of a word because most likely an ink blot would be the result. The hand rested lightly on the desk so that it could move easily along the line during long words.

The examples below are written by pupils who are not very competent and their script is distorted by entry strokes. The first one has problems with the joining stroke after 'r'. The next one uses an entry stroke mid word and overlaps the exit stroke. When the letters are wrongly formed in the first place the result is disastrous. The unfortunate pupil on the bottom line would have to go right back to the beginning with his letters. It is really unfair to burden such pupils with unnecessary complexities, and most view simpler letters with great relief. Sometimes it is just a matter of being given permission to drop something that they have been made to do, and always found difficult.

For competent writers the problem will always be that entry strokes make it more difficult, in the end to join up, not less. If the primary schools that promote such models could see the results of their teaching they might rethink their policy.

Exit strokes: a recipe for disaster

Entry strokes confuse when you change from separate letters to joined up.

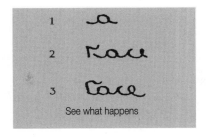

1	*a*
2	*race*
3	*race*

See what happens

tittle

100 years ago entry strokes caused trouble. They still do if you stop to dot your 'i' or cross your 't'.

care for these cats a cat petrol friends travel account they are

Decided Military,

Entry strokes overlap but do not join when you stop and start in mid-word.

little little lit butter butter little little lit

Forget entry strokes. Wait to the end of short words to dot your 'i's and cross your 't's.

determine which is which attracts against the peice need todestone

Entry strokes on wrongly formed letters make matters worse.

finish bars

'i' and 'r' push up from the base. Mock entry strokes make 'i' curve backwards.

in in in minin

Start 'i' at the top and omit the entry stroke for efficient joins.

Capital letters: last but not least

There is not much more to say about capitals than is said below. People in some professions write entirely in stylised capital letters. For architects and some designers it is a sort of trademark. For those with trained hands this might work, but for others the constant repositioning will always be a problem. Some therapists seem to think it might be better for their patients, for some reason. Maybe it is what they consider easy for infants, but even then repositioning the pencil is difficult. Modern capitals are not meant to join. You can see what it does when writers, using entry strokes, try this. Capital letters are fair game for those who want to elaborate their script, as long as it does not go too far, but they should be discouraged from using them in the middle of words however attractive they may think it is. Most likely it is a passing phase and the writer will soon tire of it.

By the time that you have read this part of the book you will understand why there are not pages of extensive photocopiable exercises. The secret of dealing with older children and their problems is in the diagnosis, the explanation. Short relevant letter sequences are usually enough to help the writer to understand what is needed. They should provide quick results without boring or discouraging anyone. The corrected letters may not transfer at once into general writing because it might slow writers down too much to be thinking of specific letters all the time instead of the content of their work. However, if you have succeeded in persuading them that it is all to their advantage to alter, and perhaps got them interested in something that has always seemed a tiresome chore, then in the end they will change.

Capital letters: last but not least

Use capital letters for emphasis and accuracy. Keep them distinctive.

ABCDEFGHIJKLMNOPQRSTUVWXYZ

G SE Briem's alphabet shows the open proportions of classic capital letters.

ELEVEN TWELVE COME HERE QUICKLY.

Capitals fall apart at speed. They start to join and soon deteriorate. Some initial capitals make legible, economical joins to the next letter – but not all.

benea comfor-bordor trade	Dear Sir, Riu She Year Em	The France on Roman Em Spanish Pope
Avoid capitals in the middle of words.	Joins pull sloppy capitals out of shape.	Some join – some do not in a fast hand.
The Top Top You can join 'T' to 'h' but not to short letters. To The Ul Yf	Let Guide The Spiro	An Do So Of
Do not join 'T' or 'I' from the base.	Separate capitals look better here.	Joins like these can save time, but do not let them get out of hand.

Part 3

Part 3

Three approaches to handwriting problems

The purpose of this part of the book is to set out a relatively simple diagnostic technique for teachers to follow. Some of you may not need to use this for long, perhaps just to confirm your own techniques. Others may need it longer as much for your own sakes as for the pupils' as you learn to tackle problems in a subject that was not dealt with during your training. As for schools, record cards might give them an accurate idea of the scale of specific handwriting problems that face their intake.

The idea that, by the time pupils reach secondary school there are a few magic exercises or a simple formula to cure all problems, underestimates the difficulties and insults both teacher and pupil. Handwriting is such a personal matter that by eleven or twelve it is too late to suggest imposing a general model on a whole school. A formal handwriting scheme would be a waste of time for the majority who have a good foundation and only have to adapt to new circumstances and priorities. Too much emphasis on handwriting can be counter-productive as it is often interpreted as urging neatness and good presentation only. It is this that makes the more insecure pupils revert to print. The emphasis should always be on a legible but fast and efficient way of writing.

So what can be done for those who have problems with a script that is inadequate to deal with the demands of their new school? Criticism of their handwriting too often sends pupils scurrying back to the safety of print or results in an even tenser cursive. Each pupil, ideally, needs a careful diagnosis of the problem that has developed, and an explanation of why. Then he or she will need individual, sympathetic help in working out a solution. This diagnosis does not take long once you have learned the techniques involved. In secondary schools a one-to-one approach may not always be practical, so this book suggests three approaches to tackling handwriting problems.

1 That you make a quick assessment, in random groups of five or six, during the first term. This enables you to pick out those with the worst problems, to promote an interest in efficient handwriting and explain the changing demands of the new school life.

2 That you pick out those whose handwriting is in most need of help, irrespective of their academic attainment, or age, and give them individual help.

3 That as a whole-form or tutor-group activity, irrespective of the year, you discuss handwriting positively, putting forward suggestions as to how pupils can help themselves to more efficient, legible handwriting. In this way you soon pick out the few with serious problems and encourage those with less serious difficulties to experiment and improve.

Part 3 can be used with any of these approaches. It enables handwriting problems to be tackled sympathetically by any member of staff. Science, History or Language specialists in secondary schools are just as appropriate as English or Art teachers; and P.E. teachers may well be best qualified to spot and deal with posture and any other physical problems. When it comes to emotional and tension worries reflected in handwriting, whoever gets on best with the pupil could be most suited to help.

Using the three approaches

1 A short text can be set to small groups and analysed later. The teacher may wish to spend the duration of the testing time observing the pupils

and making notes of *how* each one writes (posture, paper position, pen hold, etc.). These observations can sometimes suggest a quick solution.

2 Any teacher, having learned the diagnostic techniques explained in Part 3 should quickly get to the root of pupil's individual problems and be able to help guide them through the checklists, and perhaps set up a voluntary lunchtime self-help club for those with handwriting problems.

3 Any section of Part 2 can be used for class discussion, or be set as homework. Short essays on some of the points raised, for instance, on page 40 can help pupils to become aware of some of the problems, of both the writer and the reader, and to find solutions for themselves. If tackled in this way, handwriting can be made an interesting topic, not a chore.

Each of the three suggested approaches has its advantages and serves slightly different needs. A relatively simple system of dealing with the most common problems is needed first. Undoubtedly pupils with deep-seated problems will need more informed individual diagnosis and constructive back-up for some time. Problems do not just go away; they become more difficult to diagnose and cure the longer they are left.

An early survey (perhaps during the first few weeks of the new school year) will ensure that those in most need get help as soon as possible. This is where the third approach comes into its own. For some pupils, an accurate awareness of a problem will be enough. Such individuals will be able to use the relevant pages of Part 2 to spot their own faults and, by experimenting with either the practical suggestions or the movement exercises, more or less cure themselves.

This is teaching the very quality needed: self-criticism. The sooner the cure is put into the hands of the pupils themselves, the better. Older pupils certainly respond well to this reasoned approach. The confidence gained from self-motivation and self-help is soon reflected in their written work and promotes all round improvement. Plenty of adult encouragement is needed but not too much coercion.

Just a word of warning: the schemes in this book may, initially, work in the opposite direction from that which pupils ultimately need. This analytical, self-critical approach should be seen as a temporary, short-term measure for training or retraining. It can make people too aware of their writing as a technique, whereas handwriting, like so many other skills, only becomes really efficient when performed automatically. The mind needs to be free to concentrate on the content of written work without worrying about the action of writing. There is a fine balance between persuading those with difficulties to concentrate on individual letters while they are retraining, while also maintaining awareness of their long-term objectives.

To be relevant to all pupils this book has to appeal to, and cover, a wide age and ability range. It assumes, without minimising the problems, a basic level of achievement. Teachers will, however, sometimes be faced with pupils whose writing falls far below this level. A thorough programme of instruction must be applied in such cases, starting from whatever point is appropriate. The principles of such a programme should be identical to those letterforms described on page 3, dealing with movement and height differentials before tackling joins. More repetition, simpler exercises and greater supervision and encouragement will probably be needed.

■ Diagnosis

Let us start by assuming that you are seeing a pupil for the first time. You may already be familiar with his or her problems but this method will help you to look at long-standing worries with a fresh outlook and ensure that you will be able to tackle any newcomer's difficulties.

Something that the pupil has already written will help you to make general judgements. It will show up inconsistencies in size, slant or spacing. It can give you a fair idea of how tense the writer is. You may be able to detect incorrectly formed letters this way, but it is seldom enough to enable you to make an accurate diagnosis.

You *must* see the writer in action. This is the only way to judge whether the poor writing is caused by bad physical habits, an incorrect writing movement or a combination of both.

Diagnosis can be divided into three stages:

1 Observation.
2 Procedure.
3 Assessment.

Stage 1: observation

Postural problems

First observe *how* the pupil has been writing. This is just as relevant as, and has of course influenced, *what* has been written.

Let the pupils sit and write a few familiar words, perhaps their name and school. While they are doing this you have a chance to spot faults in writing posture. This term 'writing posture' is not confined to sitting up straight; it includes how pupils hold their pens, and what their wrists, arms, necks and shoulders are doing; it is dependent on the position of the writer's paper and often on the height of the chair or desk.

See pages 26-30 of Part 2 where pen hold, paper position and other practical aspects of handwriting are explained.

You need to observe:

1 Whether the standard chair is either too high or too low for the writer. Tall children may be unable to get their knees under small school desks. Sitting sideways can become habitual and continue long after the cause has been removed. Short children have more obvious problems but these too can have long-lasting effects on their writing posture.

2 Whether the pupil is able to sit straight with no undue tension to neck or shoulders. You can judge this more easily from behind the writer's chair.

3 Where the paper is positioned in relation to the mid-line of the body. This must be related to right- or left-handedness. Notice also the angle of the paper.

4 How the arm is held. Is it clamped close to the body, has to stretch across the body or is able to move freely from the shoulder?

5 How the wrist is positioned. Is it inverted or non-inverted? The angle of the wrist may determine whether the pen comes from above, the side or below the line of writing.

6 The hand position. Is it on edge, slightly flattened or perhaps excessively so? If it is too much on edge you should already have picked this up, as this usually entails a twist of the wrist.

7 The finger position. How many fingers are on the pen and is the thumb or one of the fingers nearest to the pen point? Notice the angle of the forefinger. The importance of all this is explained on page 26.

The furniture must fit the pupil. Too high or, as in this case, too low a chair prevents the writer from sitting properly. The relationship of chair to desk height is as important as chair to leg length.

Letter problems

Please read the relevant pages in Parts 1 and 2 where the letter faults are explained quite clearly.

You need to become so aware of the movement of letters that you can immediately spot wrongly-formed letters, while a pupil is writing or in a written sample.

As a quick guide to the commonest faults check:

1 Point of entry and direction of stroke.

2 Strokes that are missing from letters.

3 Letters that are the wrong height.

See also the list on page 40.

The next step is to note how much the letters are joined and how well they are joined. Check the joins, group by group, bearing in mind that 'bad' writing is often caused by poor joins.

You should then judge how consistent the other elements of handwriting are: size, slant, alignment, letter and word spacing must all be taken into account.

Notice if there is any evidence of tremor, or significant differences in line quality. These may signal a slight disability or be a sign of tension.

Tension

Tension shows up in so many ways, and has many different causes. It can distort handwriting to such an extent that it can mask the true state of affairs. You must note whether the pen is gripped excessively hard or is pressed over hard into the paper. These are the easiest signs of physical tension to spot.

You must watch to see if there is undue hesitation or changes of pressure during long or unfamiliar words. This signals, among other things, that the problem may lie in tension induced by poor spelling. (Tension caused by other difficulties such as comprehension can also show in handwriting. This confuses the issue because it suggests that the writing is at fault when there is nothing basically wrong with it.)

Uneven spacing and unexplained differences in letter size or slant can also signal extreme tension. Strokes or even complete letters can be left out. You must take great care to get the pupil relaxed before attempting a diagnosis. First of all, without the stress there may be little wrong with the actual writing. More important still, any criticism will result in more tension and further deterioration.

You may wonder why there is no reference to neatness or presentation. This would provide too general a judgement at this stage. Writing will get tidier as the faults get untangled and dealt with. Keep those untidy samples for comparison later on, but deal with specific issues first.

Speed

Speed is complex because so many issues are involved. How can you judge accurately whether a child's hesitation is caused by tension, poor spelling, lack of concentration, or the act of writing? The usual test asks a child or a whole group to repeat a phrase over and over again for several minutes. Letters are counted, averages are taken but what has been proved? Such a test will favour the ambitious pupil who will enjoy the race against the clock no matter what it does to the standard of writing. You may misjudge the more honest pupils who know what speed is best for their writing, and upset the ones with real problems. This is not going to help you much with your diagnosis.

Look at speed in a different way. Absolute speed says nothing about the speed at which a particular pupil ought to write. Each person has an optimum speed to think, and to make slow thinkers speed up causes nothing but confusion. The same applies to handwriting. If the optimum speed is exceeded the writing will fall apart. There is only a problem if the pupil's optimum speed is not being reached.

Perhaps in the early stage of assessment, only two simple questions are necessary.

1 Can you write as fast as you want to?
2 Do you feel you could write legibly any faster than you do?

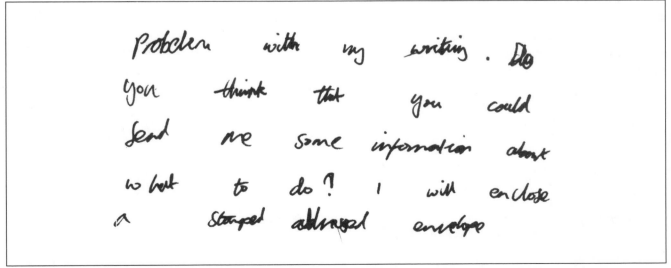

A typical example of tension and unhappiness showing through handwriting. This intelligent 14-year-old has problems that are not concerned with actual letterforms. He needs understanding and encouragement, not criticism.

Stage 2: procedure

Relaxation, confidence and motivation are all needed. In a few cases this is all that is necessary! Those pupils who have been criticised for having a personal style different from the school model, or one that offends their parents will quickly warm to sympathetic assurance. The tenseness and uneven look to their writing should soon disappear. With confidence, small, cramped writing should start to flow. To give this kind of assurance you must of course have made quite sure that there are no basic faults in the writing movement.

The first session is most important. You have made your initial observations; how should you proceed in a one to one situation?

1   Provide a good selection of pens for the pupil to try. Offer lined and unlined paper. If you give a choice then you will set the right atmosphere. Show from the start that you are on the pupil's side.

2   You can do without words or even letters in the first exercise. This takes the pressure off those with multiple learning difficulties. It also makes your job easier.

Let the pupil try the relaxing exercises on page 33 of Part 2. Read the page together or, if you prefer, you can do the explaining.

You can learn a great deal from these scribbles when you know how to interpret them. They show up hesitation, excess pressure or difficulty in producing a particular stroke. You will have to decide the exact cause but you now have a visible trace of any practical faults the pupil may have. This sample is valuable; keep it carefully so both of you can *see* the

progress as you tackle the problems. The next step is to deal with any postural faults.

Procedure for dealing with posture

1   Make sure the chair is a comfortable height; if it is not, get a cushion, move to another desk or do whatever is necessary to ensure that the writer sits up properly. Check that there is good, appropriate lighting for either right- or left-hander. If the writing surface is poor, provide a pad. Each stage in changing bad conditions, and also showing that you care, can also show improvement in the written trace. Repeat the scribble exercise and observe and discuss any differences.

2   Paper position is also important. Remember that all these practical factors are interdependent; change one and they all alter. Where you place your paper is vital because it often determines whether you can see what you are doing. Writers may need to move the paper to left or right or experiment with a different slant. Then they will be able to sit up properly, straighten the wrist or allow their arm to move more freely or correct whatever has been wrong. This simple alteration usually makes a great difference. However, it does bring into play new and unaccustomed muscles so some pupils may resist the change at first. If an explanation is not enough to convince the pupil, do not insist. It is vital to gain confidence in this first session. You must score a success somehow, so switch to a letter fault that you are more confident of solving. You can always return to pen hold or paper position at the next session.

3   Pen hold is a complex business. Forget preconceived ideas and judge each case on its

You can tell a great deal from the simplest patterns. These examples show varying degrees of tension and control. Already you have a fair idea of where each pupil's problems lie.

You need to try out these pen holds to feel why some work and others do not.

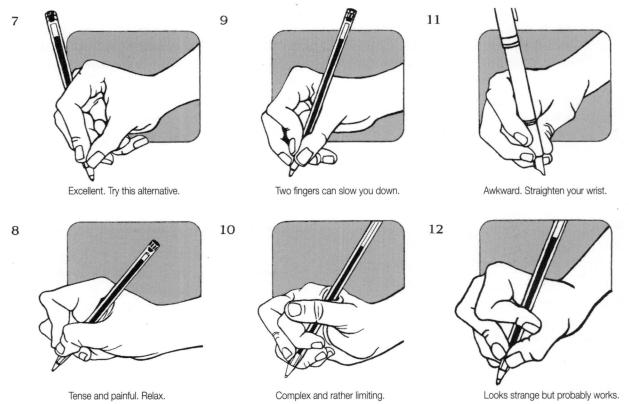

7 Excellent. Try this alternative.

9 Two fingers can slow you down.

11 Awkward. Straighten your wrist.

8 Tense and painful. Relax.

10 Complex and rather limiting.

12 Looks strange but probably works.

Some unconventional pen holds, see pages 28 and 29.

merits. Consult Part 2 and read the pages on both conventional and unconventional holds carefully. It is not sufficient to ask whether the pen hold is conventional or not. 'Does it work for you?' is a more relevant question. If a pen hold is causing pain, stopping a pupil from writing fast enough or unduly distorting letters, then something must be done.

Pain is the easiest to deal with because the benefit is obvious. Your job is to assess which element of the grip is causing the trouble; the fingers, the hand or perhaps the wrist. The principles are explained in Part 3, but neither hands nor holds conform to strict rules. You will have to work out any changes together. Remember that the writer has to *want* to change. Without motivation you cannot alter bad habits. Pupils with a problem should alter each element of pen hold in turn to see what helps them. You can discuss any changes to their writing but they must decide what feels best. Any alteration, however beneficial, may feel strange at first. You should leave the complex movements that arise in ordinary sentences until

the hand gets used to the changes. Start with the relaxing exercises then go on to simple letter patterns. Giving the writer the techniques to work out a personal solution is the best way of reaching a permanent cure.

The unconventional pen holds shown above and in Part 2, pages 28 and 29 give you more information on this complex subject. The drawings above are all taken from actual photographs. They are a sample of those you may find in any group of schoolchildren. With the exception of Number 7, they are not meant as teaching models. They can help you decide which pen holds to change and which to leave alone. But first you must understand why these pen holdss have arisen and how each is likely to affect the writer.

Left-handers, allowed to find their own solution, often clear their line of vision by manipulating their hand rather than changing their paper position. This partly accounts for the twisted wrist and perhaps the thumbs tucked out of the way. You will have to alter the paper position before you can do anything about the pen holds. The illustrations on page 35 highlight another point that is less easy to understand.

Notice how the left-handers on page 28 have used different strategies to achieve the same pen slant as a right-hander. Hands 1 and 2 have twisted the wrist so the pen comes from above the line of the writing. The top one is worse, and will be harder to change.

Hands 3 and 4 come in from the side. The top one pushes with the thumb and the bottom one tucks the thumb in. Neither is desirable, but the bottom one is by far the worst.

Hands 5 and 6 come from below the line of writing like most right-handers. The upright pen position is achieved by taking the thumb out of action. Some of this uprightness may be needed to make ballpoints work properly. Bear this in mind as you advise students.

The length of fingers can influence pen holds. Long fingers can be cramped in a conventional pen hold. Hand 7 provides an alternative which can solve both pain and pen angle.

Young children often use two fingers to steady the pencil. This happens most frequently when five-year-olds are given extra fat pencils to start with. The habit persists. When the two fingers do not synchronise as in Hand 9, there can be trouble.

It is hard to see why holds 10 and 12 evolved. An injury to the index finger is always possible.

Hand position 11 is a puzzle. Right-handers have no excuse to twist their wrist. The only cause is wrongly positioned paper.

Read the comments on these 12 pen holds in Part 2 on pages 28 and 29 as well as pages 26 and 27 on hand positions. Try out any unconventional pen hold to feel how it works before deciding whether to advise a writer to change. Remember that some people manage to write well with the most unusual pen holds, and it may be unwise to alter them.

Note: A triangular pen grip can somtimes help when changing pen hold, or, better still, a Yoropen.

Procedure for dealing with letters

Even when you are satisfied that you have isolated the letter problem, it is important to acknowledge that it may be difficult for pupils to change their habits. They may have trouble in programming a new movement or they may not even be able to perceive the differences between a correct letter and their own. Your first job will be to explain why the writing faults make it difficult for anyone else to decipher the words. It may help to trace back to how

a habit started. If you can shift some of the 'blame' onto early childhood habits and explain perhaps that it is a common problem with quick writers, you can often defuse a tense situation. You do not have to look far for a logical explanation either, though it is up to you how much you disclose! Bad handwriting is more often the result of bad teaching than any fault on the part of the pupil. A child with poor writing will probably have been subject to constant criticism. If they had received informed help earlier they might not be in their present state. You may be their last chance, and they deserve an honest explanation of their plight. When you have their confidence you have several options:

1 You can find examples of the specific fault in Part 2 and use them to explain why the fault needs to be dealt with. With sensitive pupils it may be better to focus on the sample rather than their own writing.

2 You can use the appropriate sample phrases and sentences used throughout Part 2. These sentences are meant to be used in various ways: to reinforce diagnosis, to emphasise the fault to the writer and then to practise to cure it.
Note: Pupils may well prefer to invent their own sentences.

3 You can launch straight into correcting the written sample. This is the most direct and, if it succeeds, the quickest method.

These examples, showing strokes left out, come from page 62

> When I write in this
> writing I can't read it
> to learn my notes.

Fast writing

> This is the way I
> write so that I can
> read it.

Slower writing

It is important to have examples of both fast and slower writing. Many pupils, boys as well as girls, reject the beginning of a joined hand because they judge it to be untidy. You must explain the advantage of joining and help them to develop an efficient legible movement.

Exercises

The principles of repetitive letter and word exercises are dealt with in great detail in Part 2. You will find exercises for most faults there, and will quickly learn how to make up any others that may prove necessary.

You may find that more mature pupils need only diagnostic help. If you provide them with the relevant page, they may be able work out their own solutions. Radical alterations are sometimes needed and you may worry that this will slow pupils down. This is of course exactly what will happen because when you concentrate on letterforms, writing ceases to be automatic. In this case balance the temporary inconvenience against the benefits of retraining and make sure that the pupil understands and agrees that it is worthwhile.

Be prepared for surprises. The cases that you expect to be the easiest can show up unexpected perceptual or motor problems. You may need considerable ingenuity and have to try a combination of approaches to solve them.

Be generous with praise for the slightest improvement, and do not expect miracles. Some pupils may take a long time before a new movement becomes automatic. Until then, each time the corrected letter occurs the pupil has to make a conscious effort to overcome the habitual movement. This explains why it is possible to do quite well during an exercise session but regress during creative writing tasks. The mind is concentrating on content and lets the hand go on in its accustomed way.

You need to have the co-operation of all the members of staff who deal with the pupils that you are retraining. They can give the extra encouragement that helps so much.

Group therapy

You may be dealing with groups of pupils either from choice or necessity.

Marking each other's work makes pupils realise how difficult it is to read poor handwriting. This leads to an understanding of why people criticise *their* writing. This technique teaches self-criticism but you must make sure when using it that sensitive pupils are not teased about their writing.

You will still have to give time to diagnose individually, and prescribe relevant exercises. Blanket exercises given to the whole class seldom do any good. Boredom soon sets in with those most in need of help. Copying a passage to *improve* your handwriting is even worse. It only repeats and reinforces the incorrect movements that so desperately need altering.

Stage 3: assessment

You will have been assessing problems from the start as a part of diagnosis. The more experienced you are the less you will have needed the series of checklists.

However comprehensive a checklist you have, it can be of only limited help in many situations. There are many problems that can only be judged on an individual basis. Take a typical example: whether or not to change an older pupil to cursive. A high-achieving eleven-year-old must be encouraged to join up but you will not succeed unless you can persuade the writer of the benefit of the exercise. You will need to explain that initially joined-up will be less neat and not necessarily even faster. However, with practice the resulting speed will make all the effort worthwhile. The writing will also look more mature.

Dealing with the same problem with a low-achieving fifteen-year-old is quite another thing. It might be pointless and counter-productive to attempt to alter a clear print in this situation. No checklist can help you with that assessment.

This is a good time to think again about speed. It might be useful to see how much faster pupils can write as they improve but can this ever be a real indication of success? Speed alone ignores too many of the other aspects of writing. A simple test against the clock would show if the pupil's writing speed had increased since the last test, but legibility is just as important as speed, and it will not measure that. A more efficient movement can be used to make writing easier to read.

Some older pupils actually have to be persuaded to write more slowly. There is a delicate balance between the speed and the legibility of handwriting. Go too far in either direction and you upset this balance.

Checklists, despite their limitations, have their uses at two levels:

1 To help teacher and pupil to assess the situation at the early stages of diagnosis.
2 To help assess improvement.

Assessment of improvement

There are two points to consider here: the first is why is it necessary? From the teacher's angle a record of improvement is essential. Not only is it needed for the pupil's sake, but professional satisfaction, research surveys, and quite likely school policy depend on the keeping of methodical records.

From the pupil's angle it is usually desirable to compare 'before and after samples'. It is good for morale to see improvement, and essential in helping to develop self-critical awareness in pupils.

The second point is how to set about it. This time let us start from the pupil's angle. Part 3 has been designed as a series of checklists, but the whole system is meant to be as flexible as possible. Some pupils will have needed your help at every stage, but others may have enjoyed checking in pairs or groups. The most mature, however, will have skimmed through, extracted the information required, and put it straight into use.

These three levels of pupils will have different requirements when it comes to assessing their improvement. The last group will be quite able to monitor their own progress. Their motivation to increase legibility or speed is enough once they understand the problem. Filling in checksheets is not necessary for them; it would only cause annoyance and frustration. In this case you will have to do any assessing yourself for your records. These pupils do not want to be reminded of their previous problems!

The middle group may well profit from and even enjoy assessing and marking their own improvement on specially prepared checklists. They will, however, only need those portions that apply to their specific faults. You alone can judge how much use this technique is to each individual, and how much valuable time should be used for it. It is the first and least mature group that will profit most from formal self-marking. This does not mean that they are always the worst writers, but that this method is most likely to appeal to them.

It is essential to keep written samples at every stage for you and your pupil to monitor improvement. Your own common sense will guide you on how practical it is to use elaborate checksheets. An inadequate or inappropriate checksheet is more trouble than it is worth. The difficulty in producing a practical checksheet lies in the complexity of problems that you are likely to encounter.

Checklists, despite their limitations, have their uses at two levels.

1 To help teacher and pupil to assess the situation at the early stages of diagnosis.
2 To help assess improvement.

Guidelines for designing checklists

Divide a large sheet of paper into six parts. If you find that you need more space, then spread the subjects out into eight divisions on two sheets. A section for general comments is also useful.

The way you use the first 5 parts of the checklist is fairly straightforward. Part 6 needs some thought. Use of a scale of marking is one way of tackling these aspects of handwriting. Use also for Legibility, Part 4 below.

Name _____

Form _____

Date _____

1 Posture
Body
Arm
Wrist
Hand position
Paper position

4 Legibility
Overall legibility (scale of 5)

Legibility factors 1 – 12
(Part 2, page 40)

2 Fingers
How many?
Which leads
How close to the point?
Angle of finger?
Tension
Hand/arm/fingers
Pressure on pen
Pressure on paper
Tremor
Pain

5 Joins
Baseline joins
Top joins
Crossbar joins
Joins to round letters
Overall efficiency

3 Letter construction
Wrong point of entry
Wrong direction of stroke
Strokes added
Strokes omitted
Height differentials
Descenders/Ascenders

6 General Features
Slant
Size
Spacing
Speed
Alignment
Unconventional letters
Stylistic exaggerations

Comments

Using checklists

Use of a scale of marking is one way of tackling these aspects of handwriting. Use also for legibility.

Slant

This could be measured on scale of 5.

1 Excessive backward slant.
2 Slight backward slant.
3 Upright.
4 Slight forward slant.
5 Excessive forward slant.

An additional measurement is needed for consistency.

Size

This also needs a scale of 5 plus consistency.

1 Too small.
2 Small.
3 Average.
4 Large.
5 Too large.

Spacing

This also needs a scale of 5 plus consistency.

1 Too close.
2 Close.
3 Good.
4 Wide.
5 Too wide.

Speed

This could be marked approximately on a scale of 5.

1 Very slow.
2 Slow but adequate for the writer's needs.
3 Fast enough for all needs.
4 Very fast.
5 Too fast for legibility.

Alignment, unconventional letters and stylistic exaggerations require specific observations.

Checklists for pupils

Pupils will not necessarily need to check the first two sections that deal with their writing posture. The other sections may not be relevant in every case either. Pupils need only a checklist that shows their specific category of fault. Here is an economical suggestion. Have smaller individual sheets that cover one section of the teacher's checklist at a time, to be used as appropriate. Even within a specific section not all points will be relevant to each student. Only the four most common faults should be printed on the pupil's checklist. The rest should be blank for their own faults to be filled in. This gives you real flexibility.

Marking

You need a marking system that is flexible enough for both you and your pupils. The way you mark will also vary, at different stages.

At the observation level you will only want to record errors. The pupil may use the checklist in a different way – to learn self-criticism. Marking points that are satisfactory as well as those that are wrong is a more positive approach, particularly for the insecure child.

At the second stage when you are assessing improvement, a different system of marking will be needed for some aspects of handwriting. It is the consistency of each element that you have changed that contributes to the quality of the reformed hand. A sliding scale of perhaps five or six marks might help you to judge the consistency of slant, spacing, size or even joins. There are two kinds of consistency: short-term when you are measuring it in an exercise, and long-term.

You will need to work out a system to monitor progress over a period of at least several weeks after retraining.

In the end, a complete quantitative analysis of improvement may be almost impossible.

The role of surveys and research

Small school surveys and extensive research projects can both prove valuable. They can provide, at different levels, information about what is occurring in our classrooms at any given time. Observations of relatively small groups of pupils can point the way to what is needed in specific circumstances even if this is not sufficient to influence a regional or national policy. Surveying the different features of letterforms or writing posture leads to an understanding of the complexities of the subject, but if these complexities are not taken into consideration it may limit the usefulness of any survey.

On a personal level, both surveys and deeper research can be rewarding. However little time or money is spent, any project involves delving deeper into your chosen subject and the insight gained will lead to even more informed observation. The benefits, however modest, will compound to make teachers and therapists more effective in their work, at the same time making everyday work more interesting.

It is not easy to draw the line between survey and research. Both require preliminary decisions to be made such as what to observe and how to go about the task. It is a matter of depth and time spent. To rank as research, certain precautions need to be taken to ensure the validity of your findings. The work of others in the same area needs to be consulted and compared. This might involve quite considerable reading, as well as critical comparison (you may well find that you disagree with other people's findings). Any future readers of your work will need to know the details of your methodology. Then the format for writing up research for publication may be time consuming, but do not be put off by that.

Much handwriting research is carried out in laboratory conditions and as such does not easily reflect what is happening in a classroom. There is always a difference between conscious and unconscious writing – what kind of handwriting you produce when you are concentrating on the act, and what you do naturally when you are immersed in the content of your work. If our research in the field (that is, the classroom) is to be more relevant, it is important that certain procedures are carried out. Test conditions must be precisely the same for each pupil in the sample, and the sample should be as representative as possible of any group. Then it must ensure that enough from any category of children are included to give validity and significance to your findings.

To plan and conduct a simpler survey some basic questions for you might be:

1 Should each pupil be tested individually or can the information be gathered in a whole-class situation?
2 Is any kind of questionnaire useful or necessary?
3 Should specific tasks be set or can the conclusions be drawn from what can be observed in the classroom?

For instance: a pen preference test can be carried out by handing a selection of writing implements around the classroom comprising different pen points and different sized and shaped barrels. Then pupils can write their name with each implement and mark the one that they like the best. However, investigating pen hold requires careful observation of each pupil in action. Photographs from several angles will provide the evidence you require for future analysis.

When it comes to looking at letterforms, some people use previously written examples to measure various aspects – wrongly formed letters, how many joins, etc. However, with a desirable sample of pupils of varying abilities this may prove unsatisfactory. The less able produce shorter texts with less complex words and may not include the more unusual letters of the alphabet. A set text is preferable. To get a natural example of your pupils' writing they may need to practise the text once or twice, but not more. This helps those whose difficulties with copying, spelling or even comprehension might distort the findings. It is particularly important if you are timing the work.

If you are concentrating on timing alone it is revealing to let the pupils write the set text normally and then tell them to scribble it again as fast as they can. The difference in speeds, joins and letterforms can be remarkable.

Research concerning the standard of handwriting is notoriously difficult to undertake. Take care when interpreting other people's work as the perception of what is good or bad handwriting, or whatever is being judged, is so subjective. What one person deems good handwriting another one dislikes. While one might, quite understandably, rate a mainly separate letter script most legible, another would place it bottom of the scale because of the lack of joins. While on the subject of joins, it is interesting and quite simple to count the joins used by any particular group of pupils. Inspecting a text you need to count letters that join, those that touch, those with exit strokes preparatory to joining and completely separate letters. If you compare girls with boys you might be surprised.

One of the most important surveys for any secondary school to undertake concerns pain. Just a simple 'hands up' would tell you quite a lot. A more detailed questionnaire would tell you more, asking such questions as:

1 Under what condition do you suffer pain?
2 Where is the pain?
3 How long does it last?
4 How long have you experienced pain?
5 What do you think the effect is on your work/examinations?

You might be shocked at the number of your pupils who will relate that they suffer pain when writing.

When it come to serious research it is important to take other factors into consideration. Your handwriting policy and model, if any, for a start, and how much priority your school gives to the skill of writing. There are marked differences between parts of the UK and many more between different countries. Readers will want to know how these factors relate to the conditions where they are.

This point also helps you interpret anyone else's research. Much of what is published is undertaken abroad where models, methods and attitudes to handwriting may be significantly different to those where you are. Be sure to scrutinise the methodology of other people's work, taking these and other relevant factors into consideration before you act on any findings that might prove inappropriate for your school.

Further practical information concerning handwriting research techniques can be found in R Sassoon 1993 *The Art and Science of Handwriting*. Intellect.

The typefaces used in this book

A typeface for children's reading

The Sassoon Primary project started as research with children, asking them what features of letters and spacing they liked best and what was easiest for them to read. At that time Rosemary Sassoon was studying for a Ph D in the Department of Typography and Graphic Communication at the University of Reading. She discovered that nobody had previously considered asking children for their views on the subject. It was assumed that typefaces suited to adult eyes and for adult purposes would be suitable for children. It was even doubted by some that any reliable data would result from asking children for their views. Children, however, had very definite views when exposed to the different features of the various typefaces then in use. The findings are reported in Sassoon *Computers and Typography* (1993) published by Intellect. Overall, both mainstream and special needs children chose letters with a slight slant, plain tops (sans serif) and exit strokes on the baseline. These help to clump the letters together into words. The added features were clear, friendly counters and slightly lengthened ascenders and descenders to accentuate the word shape. A suggestion of the movement of written characters was an important part of the design, Sassoon Primary was designed in 1986 when computers were only just becoming available in schools, but hardware manufacturers soon realised the benefits of installing a specially designed educational typeface in their products. Publishers soon found Sassoon Primary useful in general reading books as well as educational material. By this time Adrian Williams, a well established type designer, had joined as a partner in the project.

iltuyj
hnmr
bpk
cadgqoe
vwxz
sf

This typeface allows written letters to be arranged in stroke related families. There are also alternative letterforms.

bbfff
kkk
qqvw

These fonts are also used in 'Handwriting the Way to Teach it'

A typeface for handwriting

The features that children liked for reading corresponded with the features that were being recommended for handwriting. Print script was being phased out and more flowing letters with exit strokes were being introduced. Educational publishers were quick to recognise the usefulness of a typeface that could represent and teach handwriting yet not be a strict model. The arches of all the Sassoon letters reflect the movement of handwritten forms so, at last, letter families could be easily illustrated showing the relationship between the letters. The first publisher to use our typefaces in a handwriting scheme felt that a first teaching alphabet should be upright and so Sassoon Primary Infant was designed. This was the start of our policy of modifying the typefaces at customers' request and then adding them to our range. A sans serif version was developed for use in countries where print script is still in use, and for such purposes as captions and labelling. This is highly legible and particularly suited for reading text on screen. It was not long before teachers and publishers started asking for a joined-up version, but that is no simple matter. Rosemary Sassoon was determined that a joined-up typeface under her name should be flexible. That meant that there should be alternative forms and joins as illustrated here. There is also a facility to allow teachers to unjoin letters in the middle of long words to represent pen lifts. First of all a typeface was designed following directly from Sassoon Primary. This is now suggested for use in primary schools. A sophisticated version was designed later for secondary schools and that is used to represent joined-up handwriting in this book.

View all families of Sassoon typefaces at www.clubtype.co.uk

passes

fish

gates

mats

goats

three

flow

spots

These are some examples of the variations in joins and letterforms